Human Rights in Contemporary China

A Study of the East Asian Institute
and of the Center for the Study of Human Rights,
Columbia University

Human
Rights
in
Contemporary
China

R. Randle Edwards
Louis Henkin
Andrew J. Nathan

Columbia University Press   New York   1986

Columbia University Press
New York   Guildford, Surrey
Copyright ©1986 Columbia University Press
All rights reserved

Printed in the United States of America
Library of Congress Cataloging in Publication Data

Edwards, R. Randle, 1934–
    Human rights in contemporary China.

    "A study of the East Asian Institute and of the
Center for the Study of Human Rights, Columbia
University"—P.
        Bibliography: p.
        Includes index.
        1. Civil rights—China—Addresses, essays, lectures.
I. Henkin, Louis. II. Nathan, Andrew J. (Andrew James)
III. Columbia University. East Asian Institute.
IV. Columbia Unversity. Center for the Study of Human
Rights. V. Title.
JC599.C6E39   1986   323.4'0951   85-16576

ISBN 0-231-06180-3 (alk. paper)

This book is Smyth-sewn and printed on permanent and durable
acid-free paper.

The East Asian Institute of Columbia University

The East Asian Institute is Columbia University's center for research, publication, and teaching on modern East Asia. The Studies of the East Asian Institute were inaugurated in 1962 to make available the results of significant new research on Japan, China, and Korea.

The Center for the Study of Human Rights, Columbia University

The Center for the Study of Human Rights was established at Columbia University in 1977 to promote teaching and research on human rights both internationally and within nations. The center's activities involve all disciplines and address both theoretical and policy questions. An integral part of the university, the center benefits extensively from Columbia faculty and resources.

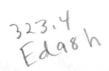

Contents

Preface

*H*uman rights is the idea of our times. The Universal Declaration of Human Rights has been universally (if nominally) accepted as a "common standard of achievement for all peoples and all nations." The principal covenants and conventions deriving from the declaration have been subscribed to by many nations, of every ideological complexion and political or economic commitment—Western and Eastern, developed and developing, democratic, authoritarian, and totalitarian, rich and poor, free enterprise and socialist.

Despite that consensus, the condition of human rights varies widely among countries, and leaves more or less to be desired everywhere. Countries differ not only in their ability or willingness to respect or ensure human rights, but in their ideological and legal conceptions of rights; in the content and scope of the rights they recognize; in their priorities and preferences when rights conflict; in how and for what purposes rights may be limited, and how much weight is given to rights when they conflict with other perceived public goods; in their institutional arrangements for realizing rights; and in their receptiveness to the influence of the international human rights movement. Countries differ, in short, not only in their acceptance of human rights as an idea, but in their entire "rights systems"—the complex of laws and institutions, social, economic, and political foundations, and ideological and cultural commitments which together determine the rights which individual human beings actually enjoy.

There has been little scholarly examination either of the nature of the international rights consensus or of the differences among national rights systems. It is taken for granted that there are ideological differences in regard to human rights between the countries of the West and those professing various versions of socialism, and that different countries of the Third World vary in the importance they assign to rights. But there are few studies of the theory and practice of rights in particular countries, and few that compare their rights systems to those of other nations, measure their performance by international standards, and weigh the influence upon them of the international human rights movement and the international law of human rights.

This study is an analysis of human rights in contemporary China seen in international and comparative perspective. Choosing China as a case study in human rights needs no special justification. China has one billion human beings, each of whom has a claim to rights. China has been an important source of ideas from Confucius and Laozi to Mao Zedong, addressing the concerns to which the idea of human rights speaks today. In our day, China has offered the world "Maoism," an ideology reflecting a conception of the proper relation of state to individual that can fairly be seen as alternative to that implied in the ideology of human rights, inviting comparison if not contrast with it.

In the mid-1980s, the human rights picture of contemporary China is hardly clear, whether from the aspect of ideology, of international politics, or of the condition of individual men and women. The People's Republic of China has not been prominent in the international human rights movement and indeed has at times aspired to leadership in the international political system on a platform that stressed not individual rights but duties, collective development rather than personal fulfillment. Yet, at least since the end of the Cultural Revolution, that message has been muted, and China's representatives have participated in international human rights rhetoric and programs. In the United Nations, notably, they have supported resolutions invoking the Universal Declaration and attacks on human rights violations by the Republic of South Africa, Chile and others. At home, the character of China's society in respects relevant to human rights has been confused, and the facts of Chinese life difficult to ascertain and comprehend. The recent period saw the rise of "Democracy Wall," then its effective demise, and the rebirth of a rule of law and of legal institutions, but hardly dedication to Western-style due process of law. One may find prominent references to individual rights in each of the four Chinese constitutions since 1954, but certainly in practice, and even as ideals and aspirations, Chinese constitutional rights differ from either the international or the Western standard. Nor can one confidently look for guidance to socialist doctrine generally, or to the ideology and practice of the USSR, for it has never been easy to identify how much of China's ideology, which of its institutions or values were socialist and in what respects they reflected Chinese traditions and ways, or whether they responded principally to the practical needs of the Chinese state as perceived by present leaders. Today, with an ideology in flux, with the measure of its commitment to socialism, to traditional Chinese ways, and to pragmatism all uncertain, and with alternating willingness and reluctance to risk exposure to Western winds and other external ideas, China is rapidly developing its national rights system, yet one would be rash to say what that system is, or where it is going. The attempt to do so here, then, must be hesitant, preliminary, and limited.

Any attempt to understand the distinctive Chinese approach to human rights would require viewing it from many angles, only some of which can be attempted here. Chinese ideas and practices that relate to rights draw on an ancient political philosophy and a long tradition of practical experience of governance which have not lost their relevance. In the nineteenth and twentieth centuries, when China began to modernize the framework of political rule, assumptions about the proper relation between citizen and state were encoded in fundamental laws by cosmopolitan constitution makers strongly influenced by Japanese and continental European theories. Marxist conceptions of law began to exert an influence during the early 1930s, as the Chinese Communist Party promulgated constitutional programs and laws in the areas which it ruled. In the last decade the Chinese government has increasingly aligned its rights position with conceptions under-lying the New International Economic Order, with its implications of priority for social and economic rights and with its perception of rights issues in terms of the international balance of economic power as much as in terms of the relative claims of individual and state.

Although we take note of these strands of influence in the essays that follow, we turn most often to conceptions of rights in the United States as a benchmark for comparison. We do not mean to imply that U.S. values embody universal standards against which all other countries should be measured. Our goal in the first instance is simply to bring the Chinese conception into sharper relief, describing it as clearly as possible to readers who will be more familiar with the United States than with the Chinese political system. Second, however, we believe that the differences between the two systems make them especially rewarding for comparison. Although every country's rights system is unique, in significant ways the comparison of China and the United States has appli-cation beyond those two countries, for each can be seen as rep-resenting a group of states, the socialist and the liberal-democratic, committed to competing ideologies.

To be sure, the United States may be unusual even among Western nations for the strength of its commitment to in-dividual rights even in competition with the public interest, indeed in seeing individual rights as itself a major public interest. China's version of socialist rights also has many features special to itself. Our offering a detailed study of one nation's rights system implies that the conventional categories of international rights debates—positive versus negative rights, civil-political versus socioeco-nomic rights, individual rights versus the rights of peoples—are inadequate to comprehend the complex reality of any nation's rights system. Yet it remains true that China and other socialist states, at least those identifying themselves as Marxist-Leninist, have much in common with respect to rights, and that what they have in common differs in important ways from what liberal-dem-ocratic states have in common. Moreover, differences in rights values at home inevitably spill over into the international politics of human rights. The choice of the United States as a comparative reference point for the description of the Chinese system, then, not only helps elucidate the Chinese system itself, but should throw light on issues that have troubled the international human rights agenda.

We therefore offer an analysis of the rights system of a nation that is one of the proudest exponents of a statist and developmental conception of rights, by citizens of a country that is prominently identified with an alternative, liberal conception. Our concern is not just to enumerate differences between the two systems. With the United States for reference, we address variations and tensions, contradictory strands, dissident and minority ideological traditions within the Chinese system, progressive and retrograde institutional developments, the conflicting demands of social groups. Our chief interest remains understanding the Chinese system as much as possible on its own terms—how it is justified, and how it works.

Our approach, in substantial degree, is theoretical, a comparison of ideas, although not without attention to the past and to the contemporary status of rights in China. The three authors address human rights in China from different perspectives.

> — Louis Henkin, a specialist in international human rights and in American constitutional law, compares the Chinese commitment to human rights in idea and content to that of the United States and to that reflected in the Universal Declaration.
> — R. Randle Edwards, a specialist on Chinese law, analyzes recent changes in Chinese legal theory and practice in order to evaluate the performance of the Chinese state in providing human rights to its citizens.
> — Andrew J. Nathan, a political scientist, focuses on the basic right to participate in self-government, and on the related freedoms of speech, press, association, and assembly, tracing their status in Chinese political thought and constitutions since the late nineteenth century.

All three authors venture to speculate on the future prospects of the Chinese rights system, but do not aim at, and do not reach, a common conclusion. Our studies provide reasons for both hope and pessimism, and express both in varying measures.

This work, we hope, will inform those interested in the state of rights in China. For China specialists, it presents some new views on the historical development and legal status of Chinese rights. It should serve also as an example of the kind of comparative study that must be pursued if the international consensus on human rights is to be better defined, areas of agreement identified and built upon, and points of difference recognized. As such, we hope, it will be of interest not only to those concerned with China in particular, but to those interested in human rights in general.

Our work was supported by a grant from the Luce Fund for Asian Studies, to which we express gratitude. The grant provided research time for each of the authors, as well as the opportunity for a three-year series of discussions in which each of us gained much from the others. It also provided research assistance and made possible an extended series of interviews. We thank those who assisted us.

1.

The Human Rights Idea in Contemporary China: A Comparative Perspective

Louis Henkin

*I*n this essay I set forth first the idea of human rights and its contemporary articulation, notably in the Universal Declaration of Human Rights. Then, because the United States was one major inspiration for the declaration and other international instruments, and because individual rights are commonly identified with United States constitutionalism, I look at the conception and content of rights in the United States as one model of contemporary human rights and as a basis for comparison. Finally, I explore how the idea of human rights has fared in Chinese-socialist ideology and sociology, in the light of the prescriptions in the "common standard of achievement" laid down in the Universal Declaration.[1]

The Idea of Human Rights

"Human rights" is a term in common use, but it is not commonly used with precision or with agreed meaning. As used in international discourse and international instruments, human rights are claims which, it is agreed, every individual has, or should have, upon the society in which he/she lives. To call them "human" implies that they apply for all human beings in every human society equally and in equal measure by virtue of their humanity; for every human being, regardless of gender or race, class or status, wealth or poverty, occupation, talent, merit, religion, ideology, or other commitment; in every society, regardless of geography or history, culture or ideology, political or economic system, or stage of development. A person may have additional rights by virtue of some extraneous qualities, such as talent, merit, occupation, citizenship or residence, or having been elected to office. But those are not "human rights," although the right of equal access to such benefits in one's own society is a human right. If these rights are implied in one's humanity they are inalienable: they cannot be transferred or waived. They are "imprescriptible," that is, they cannot be lost by having been usurped or by failure to exercise or assert them, no matter for how long.

To call them "rights" implies that they are claims "as of right," not merely by appeal to grace or charity, brotherhood, or love or friendship. They need not be earned or deserved (although some of them might be forfeited for serious crime). They are more than aspirations or assertions of the good, and are claims of entitlement and corresponding obligation, beginning in a moral order under a moral law, to be translated into political-legal rights and obligations in some applicable legal system. For many, human rights are fundamental values and ends, not implications of some original or larger principle, not means instrumental to some larger societal purpose.

Human rights are claims upon society as represented by government and its officials. They do not refer directly to rights that an individual may have against his neighbor in some legal or moral order, although rights against society may derive from such rights between persons and both may depend on the same moral principles. But those human rights which the society must itself respect it must also ensure against violation by other individuals. Human rights are limitations on what government might do to the individual; they include also what society is obligated to do for the individual. Human rights are not in contradistinction to human liberties: they include the right to be free, and not only "free from," but "free to," as well as rights to have, and to be.

Human rights are claims upon society, but they are not against society. In the ideology of human rights, the good society is one in which individual rights flourish, and the promotion and protection of individual rights are public goods. Rights are to be protected not only against malevolence, corruption, inefficiency, or error; they are often to be preferred to other public goods and cannot be lightly sacrificed even for the greater good of the greater number, even for the general good of all. Human rights enjoy at least a prima facie, presumptive inviolability, bowing only to important societal interests, in limited circumstances, for limited times and purposes, and by limited means.

When the term is used carefully, human rights are not some abstract, inchoate "good." The rights are particular and defined, familiar expressions of respect for individual dignity and substantial individual autonomy, and of a common sense of justice and injustice. Enumerated in international instruments, notably the Universal Declaration of Human Rights, they include every person's right to life, free from arbitrary killing, and to physical and psychological integrity, free from torture or mistreatment; to freedom from slavery, and from arbitrary arrest, detention, or other physical restraint; to fair trial in the criminal process; to freedom of residence and movement within one's country, including the right to leave any country, as well as the right to return to one's own country; to own and not be arbitrarily deprived of one's property; to respect for one's privacy; to freedom of conscience and religion, expression, and association; to participation in government; to the equal protection of the law; as well as, and not least, a claim to have basic human needs satisfied—food, shelter, health care, an adequate standard of living for oneself and one's family, education, work, and leisure.[2]

International human rights are not absolute. Article 29(2) of the declaration provides; "In the exercise of his rights and freedoms, everyone shall be subject only to such limitations as are determined by law solely for the purpose of securing due recognition and respect for the rights and freedoms of others and of meeting the just requirements of morality, public order and the general welfare in a democratic society." As is made specific in the Covenant on Civil and Political Rights,[3] the right to life does not outlaw capital punishment. The right to freedom from detention does not forbid imprisonment pursuant to conviction following due process of law for recognized crimes. The freedom of movement and the freedom of communication, association, and assembly are subject to limitations for national security, public order, public health or morals, or the rights and freedoms of others. "In time of public emergency which threatens the life of the nation," the rights recognized in the covenant, with a few exceptions, are subject to "derogation" "to the extent strictly required by the exigencies of the situation." However, the derogations permitted in national emergency and the limitations permitted for the public welfare or the rights of others are circumscribed. They do not permit the state to swallow up the right. Some rights cannot be abrogated even in emergency—for example, freedom from torture, freedom from racial discrimination, and freedom of conscience. Whether a derogation is strictly required by national emergency or whether a limitation authentically serves national security or public order is not for a state to decide finally for itself but is subject to international scrutiny.

The international bill of human rights does not express or reflect any particular philosophy of rights. Inevitably, it draws on a history of ideas, but it does not necessarily adopt from that history any particular conception. Clearly, the civil and political rights in the Universal Declaration drew on notions articulated in the eighteenth century—in the American Declaration of Independence (1776) and the French Declaration of the Rights of Man and of the Citizen (1789), and in English, American, and other bills of rights. Economic, social, and cultural rights as claims upon society derived from the various socialisms, and from other conceptions of the welfare state. But the rights enumerated in the Universal Declaration and later elaborated in the covenants were not linked to any particular philosophy and were couched in terms

that would not render them unacceptable or uncongenial to any
particular ideology or society. It was assumed that socialist and
even Communist states—as well as liberal, free-enterprise societies—could recognize and respect political and civil rights. It was
assumed that capitalist, bourgeois, free-enterprise states—as well
as socialist societies—could recognize and ensure the enumerated
economic, social, and cultural rights.[4] Some differences between
those two accepted categories of rights were apparent, but these
differences applied as well in societies of any complexion. Polit-
ical-civil rights can be as readily respected and enjoyed in socialist
as in "liberal" societies; in both kinds of societies, if the society
is poor, economic, social, and cultural rights might have to be
realized progressively and subject to available resources. But the
international instruments did not assume any conflict or hierarchy
between some rights and others, between one category of rights
and another. Indeed, it was frequently asserted that all the rights
in all the categories were interdependent, and any particular right
could be effectively enjoyed only if all were enjoyed.[5]

Although the international instruments reflect no particular theory or justification of rights, some principles are implied
in the concept of rights and in the particular rights recognized.
That every individual human being has rights implies that the individual counts and has recognized interests apart from the rights
and interests of any group, or of the people of the society as a
whole. It implies that there are some limits on government, even
when it would act bona fide for the good of the majority or of the
whole society. The individual, it is recognized, also has "duties
to the community in which alone the free and full development
of his personality is possible" (Universal Declaration, article 29),
but the duties imposed must be consistent with the individual's
rights, and can derogate from them or limit them only in the circumstances and to the extent provided in the international instruments.

Particular rights imply other underlying values. There
are implications of the personhood of the individual in the principle
of equality, in the right to life and physical-psychological integrity,
in the right to a private life and an inviolable zone of privacy, and

in a core of autonomy, liberty, and freedom of action and movement. In the various safeguards for a fair criminal procedure there is a conception of justice implying fairness and freedom from injustice, and implications as to the purposes of and limitations on criminal law in a just society. The freedom of conscience and religion implies a commitment to tolerance for intellectual, cultural, and spiritual pluralism; the freedom of communication implies tolerance for the airing of heterodox ideas. A commitment to some democracy is explicit in the declaration that "the will of the people shall be the basis of the authority of government," and that every individual citizen has an equal right to participate in government directly or through freely chosen representatives (Universal Declaration, art. 21). That the legitimacy of governmental authority lies in the consent of the people is implied also in the right to self-determination added in the two international covenants. The array of economic, social, and cultural rights implies a view of government as having some responsibility for individual welfare and some obligation to assure that the individual can meet his basic human needs.

Human rights are claims by individuals upon their own societies, not on other societies or on the international community. The international human rights movement has established universal, international human rights standards for states to observe, but it has not sought to replace the relation between the individual and his society with a direct relation between the individual and the international community, or to replace state responsibility and state law, institutions, and remedies with international responsibility, law, institutions, and remedies. The international law of human rights is designed to help induce national societies to respect the rights of their inhabitants. The implementation of international standards is essentially left to each state, though the meaning and scope of any rights are international questions and whether a state respects those rights is subject to international scrutiny. The condition of human rights in any society therefore depends largely on the state, and on the extent to which, and the means by which, that state respects and ensures those rights. Inevitably, the condition of individual rights in any country will depend on its commitment to the idea of rights, and on national mores and institutions, on national attitudes, policies, and social forces.

Individual Rights in the United States

Individual rights in the United States long antedate the contemporary international human rights movement, and although the scope and content of rights in the United States are always changing, the influence of international human rights on individual rights in the United States to date has been small. But the constitutional experience of the United States was a major influence on the development of international human rights, and it should not be surprising that, as to civil and political rights, there is close correspondence between U.S. constitutional rights and international human rights.

If international human rights reflect no commitment to any particular political theory, in the United States the idea of individual rights is part of a larger complex of ideas. Historically as well as analytically, it is associated with the idea of natural rights, an offshoot of natural law. It reflects a view of man as natural, autonomous, and private, deriving probably from Protestantism, particularly from the Levelers and others who asserted the absolute autonomy of the individual conscience in relation to God. The framers of the U.S. Constitution moved from individual autonomy to popular sovereignty and individual rights in a liberal society with minimal government, under the influence of the ideas of Locke and Rousseau filtered through Blackstone, Thomas Paine, and less well-known contemporary voices.

Consider the famous words:

We hold these truths to be self-evident, that all men are created equal, that they are endowed by their Creator with certain unalienable Rights, that among these are Life, Liberty and the pursuit of Happiness. That to secure these rights, Governments are instituted among Men, deriving their just powers from the consent of the governed—That whenever any Form of Government becomes destructive of these ends, it is the Right of the People to alter or to abolish it, and to institute new Government, laying its foundation on such principles and organizing its powers in such form, as to them shall seem most likely to effect their Safety and Happiness.

Before and outside society all human beings are autonomous and free. They form and join societies voluntarily—by a social contract—and the legitimacy of society derives from individual consent as expressed in that contract. By that contract individuals become "the people" and the autonomy of individuals combines into "the sovereignty of the people." That sovereignty cannot be alienated. The people determine how they shall be governed and how they shall be represented in government, the qualifications for office, the method and frequency of selection of their governors. They determine the purposes of government and the authority to be delegated to the governors in order to achieve those purposes. The authority that is not delegated to the governors for the purposes of government remains with the people; authority over the individual that is not necessary to achieve those purposes is not delegated, and the individual retains autonomy and freedom *pro tanto*. The purpose of society is to secure every individual's natural rights to life, personal safety, autonomy, liberty, and personal property. In society every individual agrees to respect these rights of other individuals. The people, and the government they create, undertake to respect and to secure individual rights through laws and institutions.

In the U.S. conception, then, the individual is central. He has a core of retained rights. His principal right is to participate with the rest of the people in self-government, and that right is sacrosanct and inalienable (although it might be forfeited by conviction for serious crime). Although it was not always so, in principle (and now in practice) suffrage is universal. Government is representative, responsible, periodically accountable. Indirectly, the people govern, according to a constitutional blueprint. But government, even the people's government, is limited. It is limited because it can act only for purposes and by means declared by the people. It is limited also by the rights retained by the individual which are immune to infringement even by the people's representatives or by the people as a whole.

Inevitably, the rights retained by the people reflect their

assumptions as to what is a good and just society. A good society is a liberal, free society. The freedoms of speech, press, religion, and assembly are not to be abridged. Property is to be respected and protected. The individual's freedom weighs heavily even against the needs of criminal justice. The individual is presumed innocent. Arrest of an individual and search and seizure of his person, his home, papers, or effects must be reasonable and warranted. His life or liberty can be taken only after a fair trial, with the assistance of counsel, before a jury. The accused cannot be compelled to incriminate himself; he cannot be tried twice for the same offense; he may not be convicted under an ex post facto law. If guilty, his punishment is not to be cruel or unusual.

    A good and just society is based on other assumptions not articulated in the U.S. Constitution or in the constitutions of its component states; they go without saying. The individual has a zone of autonomy and privacy that is not the society's business, and government was given no authority to impinge on that zone. The right to marry or not to marry, to marry a person of one's choice, to have or not to have children, to raise one's children by one's lights—these are matters for the individual's determination, governed perhaps by his god, but not by the polity, except peripherally. The individual is a person in society and before the law, with the right to acquire, own, and dispose of property, to enter into contracts, to engage in various economic or social enterprises, and to enjoy the protection of society, including legal remedies, against invasion of one's rights by one's neighbor. The individual can choose his place of residence and his vocation, generally free from direction by society. Education is compulsory for children, but thereafter how one pursues one's livelihood—as farmer, worker, professional, small or large businessman—and one's happiness are for the individual to decide. He is limited by his abilities and his resources, by opportunity and circumstances, and by the "laws" of economics and of the market, but not by societal regulation and law. The society may limit and regulate, but only at the margins. It can regulate the market and the economy, but not the individual's freedom of choice.

    The theory of individual rights in the United States is

reflected also in the jurisprudence of permissible limitations on rights. In principle, any act of government that impinges on the individual has to be justified as within the purposes for which government was created and the authority delegated for those purposes. Individual autonomy, freedom, and property can be regulated for the common safety, health, and public welfare as the people's representatives see them, but it must be shown that the regulation is rationally related to a proper public purpose. If an action of government impinges on a fundamental right—essential privacy, political freedom, freedom from racial, religious, or other invidious discrimination—that action will stand only if upon strict scrutiny by the courts it is found to serve a compelling public interest. Private property can be regulated but cannot be taken for public use without just compensation. The Constitution, and individual rights, cannot be suspended even in emergency; only the privilege of the writ of habeas corpus can be suspended, only by the people's representatives in Congress, and only in cases of rebellion or invasion when the public safety requires it.

The U.S. conception of rights has shaped the institutions and remedies for their enforcement. The Constitution—the social contract—is supreme law, binding on all branches of government. The courts, a comparatively apolitical body, enforce the limitations of the Constitution, protecting the rights of the individual against infringement by the government. Congress and the state legislatures have provided remedies against officials who violate rights. The courts have themselves built additional remedies from the theory of the Constitution.

How do human rights in the United States look from an international perspective? The internationally accepted concept of rights, of claims by the individual upon his society, is fundamental to life in the United States in principle and in fact. The rights recognized in the United States, whether in the Constitution, the state constitutions, the laws, or by established practice, are virtually identical to the civil and political rights in the international catalogue.[6] Suffrage is now effectively universal, and the citizen generally has the opportunity to vote for representatives in various levels of government. These rights are "ensured," as required by the international covenants, by a complex of institutions, notably the courts, including civil rights acts enforceable by criminal or civil process. Rights in the United States are subject to limitations: life, liberty, and property are subject to regulation, and even the freedoms declared in absolute terms in the Constitution, such as the political freedoms of the First Amendment, will sometimes bow to compelling public need. But the infringements tolerated are like those contemplated by the international instruments, and they are subject to review by an independent judiciary. In practice there are, of course, violations of rights in the United States, as the courts hold every day. But violations as governmental policy are few and short-lived, since the political branches bow to judicial command invalidating laws and regulations. The common violations are ad-ministrative, principally caused by police excesses and in many places a shameful prison system, but a reasonably effective judicial system deters violations and terminates them when any that occur are brought to court. However, the judicial system does not catch up with all violations, and often does not provide full reparation to the victim as required by the international instruments.

It is in respect of the economic and social rights that the performance of the United States has been questioned. Cer-tainly, some rights categorized as economic-social are in fact pro-tected by the Constitution. The right to work is protected, if it means the right to seek work and the freedom to choose one's work. The United States protects the right of the worker to associate in trade unions and the freedom of trade unions. Some state con-stitutions guarantee a right to education. But the eighteenth century conception of rights reflected in the Constitution does not include as constitutionally protected rights other economic-social rights listed in the Universal Declaration or in the Covenant on Economic, Social, and Cultural Rights. There is no right, surely no constitu-tional right, to "an adequate standard of living . . . including ad-equate food, clothing and housing, and to the continuous im-provement of living conditions" (art. 11), or to health care and education. There is only the freedom to pursue all of these without governmental interference and the right to have equal access to whatever benefits the society volunteers to provide.

International human rights law, however, does not require that economic-social rights be given constitutional status or legal protection, or be ensured by some particular means; all that is required is that these benefits be enjoyed in fact. In American society, the large majority have their basic human needs and other economic-social rights satisfied by individual effort supported by nongovernmental institutions and machinery, sometimes with some assistance from government. Public education has been part of American life almost since the beginning of our national history. In addition, without constitutional compulsion, for half a century now the United States has been a welfare state, providing unemployment and Social Security benefits, welfare programs, food stamps, school lunches, housing subsidies, public health clinics, and other benefits for those who need them; such social welfare programs are now accepted as and often denominated "entitlements." These programs are protected against discrimination on invidious grounds by the general requirement of equal protection of the laws, and against arbitrary administration without due process of law. As a result, almost all Americans live better than do most people in countries that recognize economic-social rights as rights and are dedicated to satisfying them. But not being constitutional rights, these economic and social benefits are not protected as constitutional entitlements, and are subject to legislative grace and to ideological and political restraints. At different times (and in different political moods), federal and state legislatures are more or less committed to such programs, and they fare less well in competition with other expenditures when the desire to balance the budget or cut taxes is dominant. In all, it is politically if not constitutionally impossible for the United States to cease to be a welfare state, but we cannot always claim persuasively that the United States is progressively achieving these rights fully, including an "adequate standard of living" and "the continuous improvement of living conditions," "to the maximum of its available resources,"as required by international human rights standards.

Critics, especially those of a socialist persuasion, often insist that despite specious conformity to international human rights standards, American society does not provide the individual the human dignity that international human rights are designed to achieve. It is said that gross inequalities of wealth, and the dependence of the individual on market forces and on his employer, render his right to vote ineffective, largely nullify his nominal freedom and render his formal equality hollow, often corrupt even the system of justice, and generally achieve not human dignity but alienation and anomie. Americans generally reject and ridicule these charges. In any event, these charges do not address the issues of this chapter. The international human rights movement proclaimed that human rights are necessary for human dignity; it did not claim that they are sufficient to achieve it, only that there can be no human dignity without them. The world has placed its faith in them and called on states to respect and ensure them. Subject to the inadequacies indicated, the United States has done pretty well.

The study of rights in the United States and its use for comparative purposes may require asking what the U.S. lesson is. Do rights in this country depend on its particular Constitution, laws, and institutions? In some countries—in Western Europe, in Latin America, and elsewhere—human rights flourish respectably under laws and institutions different from those in the United States, without a written constitution or with a different one, and without judicial review for constitutionality or with a very different review process. And some countries have copied or adapted the U.S. Constitution, its laws and institutions, yet rights in those countries do not flourish. Perhaps we should ask what has provided the conditions for rights to fare well in the United States. What does this nation have in common with other rights-respecting countries, and how does it differ from those where rights suffer. How much— of the conception, the laws, the societal attitudes—is to be credited to an individualism rooted in Protestantism, indeed in dissenting protestantisms? To an Anglo-Saxon cultural and political heritage, and particular influences (John Locke?) that weighed heavily at critical historic moments? How much of the history of rights is due to a social and political stability that resists temptations to emergency rule; to a rich and "empty" continent and successive and varied migrations; to the changing role of the United States in a changing world—in a word, to all that has made the United States what it is in other respects? Do other countries with healthy human rights conditions also have in common religious or cultural traditions emphasizing the individual? Is there a high, positive correlation between respect for international human rights and commitments to the "liberal state," and one that allows large freedom for economic enterprise? Since international human rights include the right to have society guarantee basic human needs for those unable to provide for themselves, the state must be, or be prepared to become, a welfare state. Are international human rights more secure in a liberal-welfare-market society or in a socialist society "with a human face"? And, if the particular circumstances of the United States have been fortunate and favorable for human rights, what needs to be done to improve the soil and the climate for human rights in countries lacking one or another of the favorable elements?

Individual Rights in China

The United States is a young political entity, the first new nation in modern history. Those who founded it in the eighteenth century, though inevitably drawing on their European heritage, essentially created a new society, and they believed they were establishing it by social contract. China is an ancient society. Its governance did not remain unchanged through history, and it changed again, radically, in our times. Western political ideas, including democracy, came to China in the nineteenth century, and socialism arrived in the mid–twentieth century. But both were laid over traditional ideas and a traditional Chinese society and were adapted to the needs of modern China as perceived by contemporary leaders so as to produce a unique Chinese blend. It is not easy to say how much of that blend is traditional China, how much is socialism, and how much is original—or how much is ideology and how much pragmatism.

Chinese traditions developed over millennia, assimilating many changes but reflecting important continuities. In that tradition, theories as to the beginnings of society, if it can be said to have had any, were not important and surely had no ideological significance. In the Chinese tradition the individual was not central, and no conception of individual rights existed in the sense known to the United States. The individual's participation in society was not voluntary, and the legitimacy of government did not depend on his consent or the consent of the whole people of individuals. Individuals were not equal, and society was not egalitarian but hierarchical. Confucius, for example, spoke of social relations in hierarchical sets, such as father-son, husband-wife, which were defined in terms of duties and legitimate expectations between them. The individual was subsumed in these and other relations in a familial, paternal hierarchy, and the agglomeration of families or clans was guided by the paternal emperor.

In traditional China the ideal was not individual liberty or equality but order and harmony, not individual independence but selflessness and cooperation, not the freedom of individual conscience but conformity to orthodox truth. There was no distinction, no separation, no confrontation between the individual and society, but an essential unity and harmony, permeating all individual behavior. The individual was to be yielding not assertive, and both rights and duties were negotiable and subsumed in the commitment to harmony. The individual was exhorted to engage in moral self-cultivation and improvement, both for their own sake and for their value to the betterment of society, but the improvement of the individual was not the purpose of society. The purpose of society was not to preserve and promote individual liberty but to maintain the harmony of hierarchical order and to see to it that truth prevailed. Justice was what was required by and what contributed to that harmony. The emperor was father of the people and had paternal authority; at a second level of governance, a bureaucracy, powerful but of limited jurisdiction, carried out the will of and assured fealty to the father emperor. (Weber characterized the governance of traditional China as a "patriarchal obliteration of the line between justice and administration.") Government was not a necessary evil but an essential and desirable organization to assure harmony, although the harmonious society needed only minimal government. Law was essentially penal, the instrument of the hierarchical order and designated to maintain it, though Neo-Confucian thought began to recognize the importance of law in assuring good government. Civil law was customary, and private disputes were resolved by mediation and appeal to local custom. The ordinary Chinese person did not expect state protection or state law to serve causes other than the order of the realm.

If traditional China did not concentrate on the individual or think of his status in society in terms of claims, entitlements, or rights, the advent of socialism did not bring to China any strong commitment to human rights either. Socialism is not a monolithic concept, and both in idea and in political reality the world has known numerous socialisms. But those systems committed to the essence and deserving the name of socialism have some elements in common. At least, socialism implies a commitment to the welfare of the society as a whole. The individual is not the foundation or the focus of society, though he (and his descendants) are, of course, the beneficiaries of a socialist society. Unlike the liberal state, the socialist state has a purpose—to promote, achieve, and maintain a socialist society. To achieve its purpose a socialist state owns the principal means of production, transportation, and communication; it must plan; it must organize and to some extent even regiment the people; it may require present sacrifices for the socialist future. Although in many brands of socialism there is an essential subordination of the individual to the community, socialisms and socialists have existed who had ample room for individual concerns and human rights.

Chinese socialism claims its roots in the thought of Marx and Lenin, for whom there was no place for individual rights. When they looked at bourgeois society they saw the mass of individuals—the workers—as inevitably exploited and alienated by the economic system and the conditions of employment. In such a society freedom and other individual rights are an illusion and a deception. (Marx supported rights for the proletariat in bourgeois societies as a step toward socialism. Later, Lenin declared that the democratic republic is the road, the shortest road, to the dictatorship of the proletariat.) In building socialism, individualism is an obstacle to be overcome. Freedom as commonly understood in bourgeois societies is negative, destructive, and it and other individualist assertions—indeed, the very idea of individual rights as claims against the society—do not address the true aspirations and potentialities of man in society. Man can achieve true freedom only in community. The dominant value or goal, perhaps the only right of the individual, then, is to live in a socialist society. In such a society, a person enjoys, meaningfully and fully, benefits, opportunities—call them freedoms, rights—not freedom from or rights against the society, but rights and freedoms within it, as a member of society. In the historically inevitable socialist society of the future, after the state will have withered away, individualism will have been eliminated, and it will be meaningless to speak of individual rights. All members of the society will find themselves free and fulfilled in community.

Marx's conceptions, and even Lenin's largely, antedated the birth of any socialist states. With the establishment of the Soviet Union, with the advent of Communism later to Eastern Europe and China, it became necessary to relate the thought of Marx and Lenin (and later of Mao) to actual socialist states. Though they may see themselves, in theory and in principle, as on the road to a pure, stateless, socialist society, contemporary socialist states coexist with many nonsocialist states in an international system, a system which, whatever the inexorable law of historical necessity, immediately reflects the iron laws of national interest and power, international politics and economics. Contemporary socialist states, with socialist theory far behind, have had to respond to the rise and universal appeal of the ideas of popular sovereignty and human rights. Communist constitutions serve various purposes, but their promulgation may also have been a bow to Western constitutionalism. In successive constitutions the Soviet Union, and then China, may have responded, albeit in their own fashions, to other Western liberal ideas and to the international human rights movement.

It is instructive to consider the development of the commitment to popular sovereignty in communist doctrine. The USSR

Constitution of 1936 spoke not of the sovereignty of "the people," but of the "working people," the dictatorship of the proletariat. "All power belongs to the working people of town and country as represented by the Soviets of Working People's Deputies" (art. 3). In 1961, the USSR, in recognition of the prevailing postwar doctrine of sovereignty of the people (and in part in response to national unity and patriotism during the war), declared that the dictatorship of the proletariat had fulfilled its historical mission and that the Soviet Union was now a state "of the whole people." The various constitutions of the People's Republic of China have declared it to be "a socialist state under the people's democratic dictatorship led by the working class and based on the alliance of workers and peasants." But "All power in the People's Republic of China belongs to the people." Since "the people" is apparently still defined to exclude certain "elements,"[7] there may not be much difference in coverage between "the proletariat" and "the people," but the current terminology may imply a commitment to democracy and popular sovereignty that was absent from earlier doctrine.

The influence of international ideas is also reflected in the constitutional assertion of an extensive bill of rights. Some rights were declared in the 1936 constitution of the USSR and in the 1954 Chinese constitution, but, doubtless due at least in part to international influence, rights loom much larger in the latest constitutions. The 1977 constitution of the USSR devotes some twenty articles to the rights of the citizen. In China even the 1975 constitution, product of the Cultural Revolution, declared a number of citizens' rights. The 1982 constitution devotes chapter 2 to the "Fundamental Rights and Duties of Citizens"; rights are the subject of seventeen articles, and some are included in other articles as well.

Although the Chinese polity is still undergoing change, the latest constitution is authoritative and indicates the conception of rights in contemporary China, their promised content and the limitations to which they are subject in principle, and what the Chinese government is prepared to do to ensure them.

Concerning the right of self-government the 1982 constitution declares that all power belongs to the people; that the people exercise that power through the National People's Congress and the local people's congresses; that the people administer the affairs of the country through various institutions and means (art. 2). The people, presumably, have opted for "democratic centralism," the people's congresses being responsible to the people and subject to their supervision, while state administrative and judicial and procuratorial bodies are responsible to the organs of state power that created them (art. 3).

By the constitution "the people" have opted for socialism, and the commitment to socialism permeates the constitution and its conception of rights. It also colors the other specific rights recognized by the constitution, and substantially explains those not recognized. The principal right which socialism confers is a right to live in a socialist society, and the principal characteristic of such a society is the socialist economic system. The 1982 constitution sets out that system, including public ownership of the means of production, with some limited private property. Land is the property of the state or of the collectives, but the state may take over any land. The state plans the national economy, and no organization or individual may disrupt those economic plans (art. 15). In keeping with the socialist society, the right (and duty) to work is paramount and is set forth as part of the basic system in the general principles. "The system of socialist public ownership supersedes the system of exploitation of man by man; it applies the principle of 'from each according to his ability, to each according to his work' " (art. 6). The society provides work. If the individual works, he eats.

Chapter 2 of the 1982 constitution contains an impressive catalogue of rights. These include equality before the law; the right to vote and stand for election; freedom of speech, press, assembly, association, procession, and demonstration; freedom of religious belief and practice (although article 36[4] states that "religious bodies and religious affairs are not subject to any foreign domination"); inviolability of the person; protection from arrest except by proper authority; and prohibition of unlawful detention or search of the person. The personal dignity of the individual is inviolable, with insult or slander prohibited; the home is inviolable, and extralegal search is forbidden; the freedom and privacy of correspondence are protected. Citizens have the right to criticize and to make suggestions, to complain of or expose any violations of law or neglect of duty; those who have suffered as a result of infringement of their civic rights are entitled to compensation (art. 41). Citizens have the right (and duty) to work, the right to rest, and to material assistance in old age, illness, or disability; the right (and duty) to receive an education; the freedom to engage in scientific research and literary and artistic creation. Women have equal rights. The state protects marriage, the family, the mother and child. Parents have the duty to rear and educate their minor children, and children who have come of age have the duty to support and assist their parents. Violations of the freedom of marriage and maltreatment of old people, women, and children are prohibited.

Rights in China: A Comparative View

How do individual rights as reflected in the Constitution of the People's Republic of China compare to rights in the U.S. Constitution? How do they compare with rights under the International Bill of Rights—with the Universal Declaration as elaborated in the principal international covenants?

Differences between China and the United States in respect of rights are aspects of differences in their political and economic theory as represented by and reflected in their constitutions. Unlike the U.S. Constitution, the Chinese constitution does not claim to be a contract among the people establishing the state, or a contract between the government and the people setting forth the conditions under which the people are prepared to be governed. It is a manifesto, by the leaders to the people, describing the society that exists and its institutions, and proclaiming its values, goals, and aspirations. Like the U.S. Constitution it is largely a blueprint of government, but it provides not a blueprint for a system of government as the people prescribe it must be, but a map of a government the leadership has established, the government that is or is promised. A new constitution is a new description so that the constitution will reflect, legitimate, and confirm changes that have been instituted. As regards individual rights, too, the constitution appears not to prescribe the rights that government must observe, but rather sets forth the rights which the government claims to be providing and promises to provide.[8] The preamble to the 1982 text declares that the constitution is "the fundamental law of our state and has the supreme legal authority"; all must take it as their "basic norm of conduct, and they have the duty to uphold the dignity of the Constitution and ensure its implementation." And "no law or administrative or local rules and regulations shall contravene the Constitution" (art. 5). But in the Chinese polity there is no commitment to any paramount principle to which the constitution itself must conform. Political organs interpret what the constitution means and can amend it formally when desired. No independent judiciary or other body exists to insist on an interpretation of the constitution different from that desired by the political organs, or to enforce it against high political authority.[9] If in the United States "the Constitution is what the courts say it is," in China the constitution is what the political leaders say it is.

Rights in China differ from rights in the United States in conception, in scope, in content, and in essential significance. The United States begins with the individual, and the individual remains central, with individual welfare the purpose of society. China begins with the society, the collectivity, and concentrates on general (not individual) welfare. In the United States conception, rights are goods, ends in themselves, not merely instrumental to some larger societal goal. Government therefore is limited in principle, and inherent tension exists between fear of government and some desire for more governmental services and benefits. In the Chinese conception rights are benefits granted by the society as an aspect of life in socialist society. Socialist government is not limited; it is maximal and pervasive. In the United States all law must take account of rights, and must conform to superior constitutional limitations. In China there are no meaningful constitutional limitations on what the law may provide.[10] In the United States individual rights may bow to public need, narrowly defined and democratically determined, and fundamental rights yield rarely and only to a compelling public interest. In China rights are always subordinate to the needs of socialist society and of the socialist state. Individual rights in the United States are enforced against the government and the society by an "apolitical" judiciary. In China rights, not being independent of society, cannot be enforced against society and its government, but only against lower levels of bureaucracy when they fail to give effect to society's policy to grant certain rights.

Differences in conception also underlie differences as to the rights recognized and their scope and content. In the United States the basic, inherent, constitutional rights are political and civil rights. The individual has a voice in national policy, through representatives in whose selection he has an authentic if limited say, and who are periodically accountable and subject to replacement. The individual can freely criticize government, and dissent is protected, through opposition parties, by a free press and other groups, as well as by formal remedies. Individual welfare is seen largely in terms of autonomy and freedom. Rights include a core of autonomy and freedom of choice in personal matters (marriage, family, children, place of residence), freedom of economic enterprise, choice of vocation, and the right to accumulate property. The individual enjoys freedom from arbitrary arrest and detention, the criminal law and criminal process are largely apolitical, and the individual is presumed innocent in addition to having a right to a fair trial and to humane punishment. He has effective remedies for violation of his rights. On the other hand, except for education, the individual is primarily responsible for his basic human needs and—at best—can call on government only when he cannot provide for himself. It is up to him to pursue his happiness, autonomously, in a society committed to free enterprise and a free market, a society that resists planning and is reluctant to sacrifice the present for the future.

In China, living under socialism assures the individual satisfaction of basic human needs, and society provides the individual with particular rights, the reward of fulfilling his obligations to the society. These rights include economic and socialist rights implied in the socialist system, and such civil and political rights as are conducive to socialism, that enable the citizen to participate in socialism. Socialist society assures equal access to socialist benefits and equal protection of the laws. Within, and subject to, socialism, the individual enjoys freedoms, not freedoms from socialism but freedom to maintain, protect, and participate in socialism. There can be no freedom or autonomy that is inconsistent with the needs of socialist society, for example, as to choice of occupation or residence. The individual can participate in the process of government, but the larger decisions of governance are made by his leaders. There is no right to dissent from or even to criticize national policy. The press is not a free instrument of criticism but a public instrument for education. The ideal individual is cooperative, conformist, prudent. Any dissent is isolated, fearful, and complains of corruption or arbitrary arrest, not of regimentation.

International human rights instruments reflect no commitment to any particular conception of rights, or to any particular political or economic system. Socialism and the Chinese system, therefore, are intriniscally as compatible with international standards as are free enterprise and U.S. democracy. As regards political organization, international instruments were designed to encompass Communist as well as parliamentary polities, single party as well as multiparty states. Whatever its form, however, a system of government must ensure the individual's right "to take part in the government of his country." It must express "the will of the people" which must be "the basis of the authority of government," and must be "expressed in periodic and genuine elections which . . . shall be held by secret vote or by equivalent free voting procedures" (Universal Declaration, art. 21). China's "democratic centralism" is consistent with the international standard if the people in fact have control over how they are governed, if they have the freedom and means to inform their governors of their wishes, if their governors are accountable, and if the people can effectively replace them at frequent regular intervals. Government by bureaucracy, surely government by appointed or self-appointed elite, is not government by the people, if, though political authority is couched in legal forms and decorated with occasional formal votes, arbitrary power in fact prevails, without meaningful accountability to the people and meaningful opportunity for the people to terminate or control the exercise of such power. The Chinese system, it appears, offers the individual some opportunity to be part of the process of government, but not a voice in decision-making or control of decision makers.

In one important respect the Chinese system clearly does not satisfy the requirement that the will of the people be the basis of authority. For, it is admitted, the people of China are not free to abandon socialism. "Sabotage of the socialist system by any organization or individual is prohibited" (art. 1). Individuals and political parties are not free to speak against socialism or to seek to move the country to abandon it.[11] This is surely not consistent with the essential sovereignty of the people and their right to govern themselves. In principle, the people of the United States are free to choose any political-economic system, even to reconstitute themselves as a socialist state; in China the people are not free to abandon socialism.

The other rights enumerated in the Chinese constitution correspond to most of the rights recognized in the Universal Declaration. There are, however, important divergencies. The international human rights instruments require the state to respect the human rights of all persons subject to its jurisdiction. The rights in China's constitution are rights of citizens, not of persons. This suggests that noncitizens are guaranteed no rights, and citizenship itself is not constitutionally guaranteed, so that a person who is not accorded, or is deprived of, citizenship is promised no rights at all.

International standards may be offended also by the linkage of rights to duties and the subordination of rights to socialism. "Every citizen enjoys the rights and at the same time must perform the duties prescribed by the Constitution and the law" (art. 33).[12] "The exercise by citizens of the People's Republic of China of their freedoms and rights may not infringe upon the interests of the state, of society and of the collective" (art. 51).

Citizens of China, then, enjoy only "socialist rights," and any rights only insofar as they are consistent with socialism. The exercise by citizens of any rights or freedoms—say, freedom of speech or assembly—must not be to the detriment of socialism, of the socialist state. That does not satisfy international standards. The limitations permitted by international instruments set up an international standard subject to international scrutiny. The Universal Declaration contemplates only such limitations on rights as are necessary to secure the rights of others and to meet "the just requirements of morality, public order and the general welfare in a democratic society." In a democratic society, it was clearly recognized, public order and the general welfare permit small specific limitations on rights; they do not permit limitation that would swallow up rights or make them wholly subordinate to the perceived general welfare. Rights may not be limited for just any state interest, nor can a state insist that what is required by socialism is required by "public order" in a socialist state, for that would destroy the very idea of rights.[13]

Another discrepancy between the Chinese constitutional commitment to human rights and international standards may be buried in the constitutional emphasis on legality. Many rights are declared to be protected by law. Provisions demanding legality, implying that officials, bureaucrats, and police cannot act by personal fiat, support the right to self-government and help secure other rights. But the Chinese constitution suggests no limitations on what the law may provide. It is only unlawful detention, unlawful search of the person, or intrusion into a citizen's domicile that are prohibited (arts. 37, 39). The privacy of correspondence is subject to censorship in accordance with procedures prescribed by law (art. 40); a trial may be closed to the public in special circumstances "as specified by law" (art. 125). International standards require that limitations on rights be imposed by law (see, for example, art. 12[3] of the Covenant on Civil and Political Rights), but they require also that the law itself conform to basic human rights standards.[14]

Certain human rights are not recognized in the Chinese constitution. Chinese socialism apparently claims the right to regiment the individual for the collective good. There is no mention of any freedom from slavery or forced labor; there is no right to choose one's work, and the duty to work is coupled with a provision that the "state encourages citizens to take part in voluntary labor" (art. 42). The constitution proclaims no freedom of residence or of movement within the country, or the right to leave the country or the right to return. There is no mention of freedom from torture or other inhuman or degrading treatment. Apparently arrest or detention may be arbitrary, unreasonable, so long as it is by proper authority and in accordance with law. "The accused has a right of defence," and trials are public except in special circumstances (art. 125), but there is no presumption of innocence, no privilege against self-incrimination, no constitutional right to counsel.[15] People's courts are not subject to interference by "administrative organs, public organizations or individuals" (art. 126), but are responsible to political bodies (art. 128). And the constitution (art. 80) gives the president of the People's Republic of China the power to proclaim martial law, which would presumably include derogation from rights generally, but there are no limits to guide him or procedures to follow.[16]

Deficiencies also exist in the provisions for assuring respect for individual rights. The International Covenant on Civil and Political Rights requires that states parties "respect and ensure" the rights recognized in the covenant, and "take the necessary steps" to give effect to them. The state must assure "an effective remedy" to any individual whose rights are violated. Under the Chinese constitution, no promise of remedies assures the enjoyment even of those rights that are recognized. The constitution exhorts the political organs to respect constitutional rights (art. 5), but no judicial or other remedies prevent their violation by the high organs of state, and the remedies implicit in the political process and in democratic centralism do not seem sufficient to ensure individual rights. Unlike previous constitutions, the 1982 constitution does not provide even for appeal to a procuratorate against violations of rights by the bureaucracy.[17] Apparently the only remedy for violations of rights is that "citizens who have suffered losses through infringement of their civic rights by any state organ or functionary have the right to compensation in accordance with the law" (art. 41).

Of course, it may be that the People's Republic of China does better in respect of human rights than its constitution promises, as does the United States, for example, in respect of economic-social rights, protection against invidious discrimination by private persons, and remedies to protect individual rights. In China the government has indeed, occasionally, opened additional areas of life to individual autonomy and liberty. But, on the available information, it appears that rights not promised—for example, freedom of residence, choice of work, freedom from forced labor— are not in fact enjoyed; that rights promised—effective participation in government, political freedoms—are in fact limited by the perceived needs of socialism, of the Chinese state, or of the current government. And it appears that there is still an extrajudicial system of "reeducation" in labor camps, and a number of people are still excluded from full citizenship and therefore from rights.

China and other socialist states have made a small step toward recognizing limitations on governmental authority by proclaiming the sovereignty of the people, but that theoretical commitment has not yet been translated into some sovereignty—rights— for individual members of the people. Both in the Chinese tradition and in socialist ideology, rights are granted, not inherent—granted by government to serve societal purposes, not retained by persons as their right, regardless of the wishes of government, as ultimate values not as means to other ends.

The implications of that conception should not be exaggerated. In the United States, too, freedoms and democracy are often justified by instrumental reasoning, that they promote truth, or prosperity, or good government. In the United States, too, no rights are absolute, and virtually all rights may be sacrificed if the public need is great enough. But it makes a difference whether one starts with the individual, with his/her freedoms and other rights; whether one begins with rights as a given, and as a primary good in a good society; whether one requires that authority justify invasion of rights; whether that justification is subject to review by some more or less independent, apolitical, impartial body, such as the courts.

That rights in China are not seen as inherent, that one accepts and values them only as instrumental to societal needs, need not be fatal to respect for rights. International human rights instruments do not require ideological commitment, or acceptance of any particular basis for human rights, only that specified rights be respected and ensured, for whatever reason, or for no reason. Surely, there are instrumental reasons in various conceptions of the good society for respecting many of the internationally recognized human rights, including maintaining internal tranquility and popular support, the advantages of pluralism, the benefits of criticism, the maintenance of common culture. There has been insufficient effort either inside or outside China to persuade the Chinese authorities of the societal usefulness of rights.

The Prospect for Human Rights in China

Why is China deficient in important ways in respect of human rights? What are the prospects for improvement?

In describing human rights in the United States, I suggested the need to explore the traditions that shaped the conception of rights; the economic, demographic, and other societal factors that may have favored commitment to that conception; the relevance of happy geography and history, of congenial culture, of wealth and open space, of international power and peace. For China, too, analogous factors need study if the condition of human rights is to be appreciated and their future intelligently appraised. I have looked at human rights in China with the eyes of a United States constitutional lawyer, in the light of prescribed international standards that have Western articulations and a heavy Western cast. But in addition to examining the formal laws and institutions of China, it is necessary to probe systemic or societal characteristics and economic or sociological factors that explain China's constitutional and other legal dispositions, institutional arrangements, official behavior, and individual willingness to assert rights or to acquiesce in their denial.

China has adopted a constitution and the idea and the language of rights. Do the same words mean the same thing in the Chinese language and in China? How significant is the constitution in the life of China, how significant is the inclusion of human rights in the constitution? Has the international human rights movement seeped into Chinese awareness, or are concessions to it merely formal and diplomatic, for foreign consumption and to respond to some international clamor? The word "rights" apparently is not in common use in China, and the rhetoric of international human rights is seldom invoked there. Are other international influences more compelling, such as the abiding influence of Soviet Russian ideas and the rhetoric of the Third World in which China once aspired to leadership—ideas less concerned with the individual and with human rights than with exalting national purposes to which the individual must be subordinated? Does resistance to the terminology of human rights reflect rejection of natural law and universal ideology in favor of isolationist, egocentric preoccupations? Is resistance to the terminology of rights rooted deep in Chinese thought and life, resistance which socialism has only confirmed? How significant is it that even while constitutional promises are extant, leaders can apparently readily interpret or disregard them, individuals and groups hardly assert them, and a Cultural Revolution can destroy rights and all that they aspire to? Does the continuing sense of emergency—international beleaguerment or dire economic straits—provide a permanent reason for derogating from human rights commitments?

In some respects, no doubt, the condition of human rights in China in recent years reflects current instabilities and difficulties like those that have troubled human rights in other countries. Some reasons why China is deficient in important ways in respect of human rights are to be sought in Chinese traditional attitudes and her brand of socialism.

In significant measure the condition of human rights in China reflects resistances in Chinese tradition. Traditional China did not emphasize the individual and individualism, and although self-cultivation was encouraged, one's individuality was not to be flaunted or asserted. The contours of individuality, of the individual's proper domain and where it met another's, were not clearly marked. Man was a social animal, living in a series of hierarchical relations in a hierarchical society. The ideal was harmony. At bottom, it was thought, the interests of all individuals harmonized rather than conflicted, and institutions should reflect and seek that commonality of interests. As regards the polity, although there was no commitment to maximal government, neither were limitations on government sought. In Chinese tradition men (including governors) are good; there was no need for external limitations on them, and surely not for means to enforce such limitations.

Chinese traditions also affect attitudes to particular human rights. The notorious effort of Communist China to dispense with a legal system and to rely on informal communal mediation and accommodation may have responded to Chinese traditions more than to socialism. The recent decision to restore a legal system and the character of the legal system being restored may also prove Chinese as much as socialist. With respect to rights in the criminal process, for a notable example, even before Communism the Chinese would not have accepted the Western protestation that it is desirable to have institutions and practices that might allow ten guilty men to go free rather than have one innocent man convicted. The Chinese believed that no single guilty person should go free and no single innocent be convicted. They believed that truth could be and should be ascertained and had confidence in the methods available to them for ascertaining it. They desired confession as the best evidence as well as to serve an essential moral-educational function.

China's particular brand of socialism may itself respond to her traditional attitudes. In any case, it is an additional source of resistance to respect for international human rights. Its commitment is to a concept of individual rights which is subordinate and incidental to other goods, instrumental to the good socialist society. No high value is placed on the individual, his/her autonomy, liberty, property, security. Rather, there is commitment to and a high value on central planning and decision-making, extending to matters on which international standards require substantial autonomy—for example, occupation and residence, marriage and family size. China has also believed in sacrificing some for others and for the group, the present for the future. Unlike international human rights, moreover, Communist doctrine apparently does not accept any independent concepts of justice as a priori limitations on government, rejecting "justice," like other natural law, as the new mythology of the bourgeoisie (as religion was the old mythology). Indeed, for some socialist theory the only natural law is the law of historical necessity. In the Communist state, socialism is justice: what is required by socialism, what contributes to socialism or serves the interest of the socialist state is just, fair, desirable.

To the extent that improvement in human rights in China depends on modifications in Chinese socialist dogma and in Chinese traditional ways, the prospects for major changes are not bright. But like other socialist states, China has been blurring ideology and has been developing its conceptions of rights as it goes along, adapting them to contemporary circumstances and needs. And those include the exigencies of life in a world that responds to now universal ideas, among them human rights. In many respects, moreover, China—traditional as well as socialist— shares universal conceptions of justice. If theorists of socialism may once have insisted that there is no justice independent of socialism, Chinese theorists of Chinese socialism might insist that of course a socialist society has to be just. In China, too, there are procedures designed to render it likely that the innocent will not be convicted, because common principles of fairness and justice are rooted deep in the Chinese tradition; because unequal justice, or convicting the innocent, is irrational, unscientific, and does not ordinarily serve socialism or the socialist state; because violation of those principles is offensive to the citizen at home and brings discredit to China and Chinese socialism abroad.

Even if China moves farther from its brand of socialism than now appears likely, there is little sign that the change will soon bring freedom or that there is likely to be a transformation of

Chinese society that would abandon traditional values and make
the individual human being the focus of societal concern. But while
the U.S. commitment to human rights is highly individualistic,
international human rights demand no particular ideological commitment, only a willingness to respect and ensure particular, defined, freedoms and immunities, privileges and benefits—generally those articulated in the Universal Declaration of Human Rights.
Such willingness may have to overcome traditional, systemic resistance, but requires no radical transformations. Surely, it does not
require wild optimism to hope for, perhaps even to expect, improvement in China in respect for those fundamental human rights
which all systems accept and which are congenial to the Chinese
tradition of enlightenment and humanity in government—greater
respect for the physical-psychological integrity of the person, greater
safeguards against politicization of the criminal process, some en-
largement of the sphere of individual autonomy, perhaps even
some freedom of political expression, as well as some procedures
for ensuring these safeguards.

The path to full human rights for China may be longer
than for some other countries. Important societal needs in China
combine with traditional and socialist tendencies to tempt authorities to adopt totalitarian policies that are uncongenial to individual rights. But the idea of rights is in the zeitgeist, national
borders are permeable to ideas and to examples of other ways that
have international sanction and domestic appeal. If greater freedom in China depends on further economic development and
modernization, Third World spokesmen have recognized that the
latter cannot flourish without freedom, and only political and social
development can fuel economic and industrial modernization. There
is some reason to hope that that lesson, and the lesson of the
human and national tragedy that was the Cultural Revolution, may
yet accelerate progress toward human rights even in traditional,
socialist China.

I have compared human rights in the United States and
China in the light of international standards, and to compare is to
contrast. It is instructive also to stress similarities, convergences.
It is significant, surely, that socialist states like liberal states now

subscribe to a common credo, the affirmation of human rights. It is significant, in turn, that liberal states like socialist states recognize claims upon government to assure at least the basic human needs of the individual. The reciprocal influences continue under international auspices and the international rights banner. Earlier in this century China was exposed to U.S. and Western European influence. Socialism, too, has European roots and even when engrafted in China on other traditions brings with it some of the values that have shaped laws and institutions in Europe and the United States. China has also sought improved relations with the United States; it continues to aspire to leadership in the Third World. New openings in China inevitably expose it to strong prevailing winds, including those of the International Human Rights Movement.

In the United States the emphasis on the individual and the idea of rights existed from the beginning, but the United States became the rights society it is, gradually, over 200 years. Traditional China did not attend to the individual, and did not have the idea of individual rights; Marxism only confirmed that tradition. But early in the twentieth century the central role of the emperor was given instead to "the people," and Chinese socialism has confirmed that change. If in the United States the move was from the individual to "the people," might China come to recognize that the people is a billion individuals with dignity and rights?

In principle, at least, the People's Republic of China has come a long way from the hierarchism of traditional China; it has also come a distance from earlier socialism, including its own. It has moved toward Western ideas—the sovereignty of the people, parliamentary forms, voting. It has accepted the human rights idea, if only in the form of citizens' rights. It is part of an international socialist movement which includes examples of socialism "with a human face," warranting hope that in China, too, the individual, the living human being—not abstract socialist man, not future generations—will come to be seen as the central concern of socialism as he is of the liberal welfare state and of international human rights.

2.

Civil and Social Rights: Theory and Practice in Chinese Law Today

R. Randle Edwards

*R*espect for individual rights is closely associated with formal legality. While laws can exist without respect for rights, rights cannot long exist without laws. It is hardly surprising, then, to learn that during the ultraleft antilaw period from 1958 to 1978, individual rights in the People's Republic of China were wantonly disregarded, with millions of Chinese citizens— including many current Party and government leaders—suffering torture, unjust imprisonment, or other mistreatment. Nor is it surprising, in view of these tragic events, that since 1978 the Chinese government has begun a major campaign to establish a comprehensive and formal legal system, replete with codes, lawyers, and public trials.

I would like to express my appreciation to the Dana Fund for International and Comparative Legal Studies for the generous grant that enabled me to initiate the research culminating in this chapter.

The progressive elaboration of a comprehensive legislative structure, the training of thousands of defense lawyers, and the launching of a major public legal-education movement have made the Chinese citizen perhaps more aware of his rights and of his remedies in case of violation than ever before in Chinese history. Yet many foreign observers are skeptical that these current developments in PRC law will lead China into the mainstream of enforcement of international human rights. Some doubters argue that deeply implanted cultural traits preclude the development in China of individual rights similar to those enjoyed in the United States or proclaimed in various international covenants. Other skeptics maintain that the PRC's adherence to collectivist and instrumentalist socialist conceptions prevents the growth of genuine individual rights.[1]

It is true that for millennia China stressed neither formal legality nor the importance of the individual. Collective interests were favored over those of the individual, while the virtues of obedience, harmony, and conciliation stifled the growth of rights consciousness and adversarial litigation. It is equally true, however, that the situation of individuals in the West was not much better a few centuries ago. In other words, individual human rights are a product of historical development. Thus, given favorable conditions, individual rights may well take root and flourish in China.

This study will first consider the human rights implications of certain values that have characterized Chinese political-legal norms and dispute resolution procedures over the centuries. In the light of these values, it will then survey Chinese Communist constitutional and legal provisions pertaining to key civil and social rights. (Political rights form the subject of essay 3 of this volume.) The chapter will also selectively discuss actual rights practice in the PRC, on the basis of personal interviews, published reports, and the author's impressions from a number of trips to China.

Any society's political and legal institutions reflect the dominant values of society and the common goals that unite the society and guide governmental activity. The actual rights enjoyed and social duties assumed by individuals are determined as much by unstated but widely shared values and customs as they are by officially promulgated policies. The net impact of these underlying assumptions and ingrained habits may be to expand the rights enjoyed by the average citizen beyond those promised by the constitution and other written laws—as in the United States—or, instead, it may be to limit such rights. I turn first, therefore, to a discussion of values that shape the Chinese understanding of rights provisions in law.

Chinese Legal Values: Five Themes

Five themes permeate Chinese thinking about the individual, society, the state, and the role of law. Some of these themes have existed for millennia, while others have emerged more recently, as a reaction to internal needs or in response to foreign ideas and forces. All constitute significant elements in the conceptual framework within which individual rights of Chinese citizens are implemented. An examination of these themes will facilitate our inquiry into the nature and origin of Chinese rights and will help to guide us in our speculation about the future prospects of rights in China.

First, China's leaders have a mission—to achieve communism through rapid economic development while maintaining adherence to socialism. Policies in all sectors and the aspirations, endeavors, and acts of individuals are evaluated in terms of their anticipated contribution to the overriding goal of development, often phrased in traditional terms as enhancement of the wealth and power of the state. Individual rights are seen not as ends in themselves but as instruments for the attainment of broader social and political aims. While individual, or "citizens'," rights have been the subject of considerable attention by the Party, and by scholarly commentary,[2] they have had to share the limelight with calls to strengthen social unity and to make personal sacrifices to advance socialist modernization. Just as most Chinese feel that a woman's right to freedom of divorce must sometimes yield to the society's interest in stability of the family, likewise the due process rights of accused criminals are usually construed in terms of the prevailing priorities of the state. For example, when the Party decides to crack down on crime, procedural protections such as the requirement that the Supreme People's Court approve death sentences may be suspended to facilitate swift punishment.

Second, most Chinese view society as an organic whole or seamless web. Strands in a web must all be of a certain length, diameter, and consistency, and must all be fitted together in accordance with a preordained pattern. Nonstandard strands, or randomly stitched threads, detract from the symmetry and strength of the web and diminish its capacity to perform its function. Likewise, in both the traditional Confucian ethic and current Communist morality, the individual should conform to a standard model of behavior, characterized by an overriding concern for the interests of society and a readiness to perform the role assigned by the Party and responsible state organs.

Unlike the American conception of society as an agglomeration of atomistic individuals whose diverse and often conflicting interests are a source of strength to be protected and even encouraged, the prevailing Chinese view sees diversity of behavior as a symptom of declining morality and ineffective government. While U.S. courts are forums where the state passively presides over a "fair fight" between conflicting and usually self-serving views of fact and law, the Chinese courts, administrative agencies, and informal neighborhood organizations strive to achieve a result that will promote the harmony, strength, and prosperity of the entire society. The dominant Chinese attitude is that a perfect harmony of interests is possible and can be achieved through individual self-restraint and proper guidance by the Party. The hope is that each individual will function properly as a cog in an ever more efficient social machine. This perception holds obvious implications for the interpretation and application of particular "citizens' rights" stipulations.

Third, China's leaders today, like the imperial and bureaucratic rulers of the past, hold that rights flow from the state in the form of a gratuitous grant that can be subjected to conditions or abrogation by unilateral decision of the state. In the "feudal" period, certain regularities of judicial process served to provide some promise of fair trial, but the traditional state's principal motive was efficient administration and political stability, not concern for the rights of the individual. Likewise, the Chinese state today grants the rights of citizens in part to promote stability and productivity.

Nonetheless, the average Chinese citizen or government official probably regards the state as subject to both procedural and substantive limitations, at least in theory; it is not considered free arbitrarily to deprive citizens of their life, liberty, or even property. Though transgressions have occurred during periods of political turmoil, the Party and government have subsequently disavowed such invasions of basic individual rights and have called for redress of grievances, compensation for injury, and the perfection of laws to prevent repetition of similar violations in the future. Even under the feudal legal system, deprivation of life or liberty through an arbitrary abuse of the judicial process violated commonly held conceptions of justice and often led to persistent demands for redress.

Both regular and special review procedures have been established, in the past and today, to ensure the state's adherence to popular expectations of fair judicial process. For example, in the realm of property rights in the PRC, while the state has frequently modified the scope of legally protected interests, the principle of compensation for expropriation has always been recognized—sometimes retroactively—with the exception of confiscation of estates of landlords and rich peasants during the land reform movement in the early 1950s.

Fourth, it has never been popular or customary in China to settle disputes in an adversary manner through the judicial process. In liberal Western societies, the availability of open and independent courts for vindication of violations of individual rights secures their enjoyment and contributes to a general sense of rights consciousness. Regular resort to the judicial process for interpretation of constitutional and statutory provisions also clarifies the meaning of existing provisions of law. In addition, resort to the courts increases the degree of conformity to such unified standards on the part of executive organs and agencies. Finally, close judicial scrutiny of the constitutionality of legislation forces legislative bodies to be more careful about avoiding infringement of individual rights as they go about their task of developing new law.

But in China formal litigation was always deemed unseemly and disruptive of social harmony. The recent law reform in China recognizes the importance of public judicial protection of rights. Developments in legal education, legislation, court expansion, and public awareness of law are all quite promising. At the same time, however, a lack of judges and lawyers and the Party's stress upon unity and stability have led to a renewed emphasis upon mediation by neighborhood committees and judges, and extrajudicial sanctioning by police and administrative superiors. Resort to the courts remains disfavored by most Chinese. Disputes are most often settled through "friendly consultation" between the parties, or mediation or conciliation by administrative bodies.

One result of the prevalence of mediation has been to make even the most fundamental rights negotiable. Their enjoyment, and indeed their operational meaning, is determined through face-to-face negotiation, mediation, or settlement by direction of an administrative superior. In many cases, the last word in interpretation of laws and policies has been the opinion of the local Party organization. Its decision is essentially a moral or political statement and not a carefully reasoned legal opinion. Moreover, it can be appealed only through political channels. Although current policy prohibits direct Party involvement in judicial matters, ingrained habits and the shortage of qualified judicial personnel mean pervasive Party involvement in legal affairs is likely to continue for some time.

Because of the prevalence of mediation and conciliation, settlements in individual cases are usually ad hoc and do not serve as precedent. Like cases may be decided in myriad unlike ways, so that there is no official or unofficial consensus as to the meaning of constitutional and statutory rights. Instead of the clarity of definition that comes with judicial interpretation, mediation and conciliation contribute to lack of consensus as to the precise boundaries of rights and responsibilities. Thus a combination of traditional values and pressing considerations of current administrative necessity inevitably slow the pace of China's transition toward the rule of law.

Finally, formal procedural law in the PRC, and in traditional China, established a hierarchy of courts and a system of rules prescribing explicit guidelines for original jurisdiction, automatic review, and appellate jurisdiction. But in practice, the real rule in Chinese legal process has been a principle of nonfinality. As long as an individual continues to feel aggrieved, he can always seek yet another review from the ruling authorities.

This persistent tradition reflects two important features of the Chinese concept of justice that directly pertain to this analysis of the present status and future prospects of rights in China. First, the reluctance of China's rulers to enforce statutory limits on legal review reflects a sense that genuine justice should be served at whatever cost to administrative regularity and efficiency. A related feature is the preferred place accorded to substantive justice over procedural justice. Truth is regarded as unitary and knowable. Guilt is essentially subjective, not objective: it must be established by determining the state of mind of the accused when he committed the alleged crime. Absolute accuracy is not only possible but obligatory, whatever the means. Giving a complainant or an accused his "day in court" is not enough, nor is it even necessary if a substantively accurate and just outcome can be achieved in some other way. These considerations help explain the great importance the Chinese legal process has long accorded to the confession of the accused. Although the present code of criminal procedure in the PRC "strictly prohibits" coerced confessions and provides for conviction without a confession, in practice the testimony of the accused still plays a major role.

Constitutions in Chinese Communist Law

The first Chinese Communist rights guarantees were set forth in the "Draft Outline Fundamental Law (Constitution) of the Chinese Soviet Government" in 1930.[3] Since then, constitutions have continued to be the principal locus of rights stipulations in Chinese law. The third essay in this volume identifies the major Chinese Communist constitutional texts. The most recent of these, the 1982 constitution, forms the focus of the rest of this chapter. But what is the role of the constitution in Chinese Communist legal theory and practice?

Skeptics abound. Thus one scholar, Leo Goodstadt, said of the various Chinese constitutions that the author of their "peculiar style" was not Mao Zedong but Joseph Stalin, who stated in 1936 that "[the] constitution is a summary of the path that has been traversed . . . an historical document dealing with the victory of socialism."[4] Goodstadt concludes that the 1978 Chinese constitution is "a statement of principles which the legal draughtsman is to incorporate into laws and decrees."[5] Jerome Cohen, commenting on the same document, ascribed to it several functions: legitimization of the current government and reaffirmation of its continuity with the PRC's first generation; service as a symbol of national unity; articulation of basic goals and policies; allocation of government power; and stipulation of certain human rights. Cohen adds that a PRC constitution is not what the Western liberal tradition would call a constitution, "for it is a formalization of existing power configurations rather than an authentic institutional framework for adjusting relations among political forces that compete for power."[6]

Cohen notes that the gap between constitutional guarantees and Chinese social reality had been almost eliminated in 1975, not by enhanced enforcement but by elimination of a number of rights of Western origin. He concludes with the suggestion that

it is not impossible that the present constitutional institutions, norms, and values may give rise to practices and expectations that will develop authentic roots in China's political culture. It is conceivable, for example, that the rights to strike and to put up big-character posters may turn out to be more than tools to be manipulated in the intra-Party struggle. Such actions have sometimes been the vehicles of genuine, spontaneous protest."[7]

Ironically, both of these rights have since been eliminated from the constitution. The right to post big-character posters, associated with the now banned "Democracy Wall" in Beijing, was excised by special amendment to the state constitution in 1980, and the right to strike was excluded from the 1982 state constitution. Nonetheless, the net effect of Chinese constitutional development in recent years has been to define more explicitly the powers of governmental organs, to promote more democratic forms of political participation, and to expand the scope of citizens' rights.

Recent political developments in China, together with academic discussion over various constitutional questions, signal the importance of the current PRC state constitution, which was promulgated in 1982. It is both a major political statement and a charter for enhanced reliance upon law. One important reason for beginning a revision of the state constitution in September 1980, just two years after the enactment of the previous one, was to legitimize and consolidate the political victory won by the "modernizers" of Deng Xiaoping's group over those to his left by excising various "ultraleft" provisions such as the "four great freedoms."[8] However, other purposes were to expand the protection of citizens' rights and to enhance "socialist democracy" by increasing the power of elected organs, making government agencies more accountable to the people's representatives, and restricting Party involvement in government administration. The length of time required for the constitutional revisions, coupled with reports of serious policy differences at the highest levels of the Party, support the view that the constitutional revision was not easily achieved. Respectable journals even printed arguments calling for retention of the right to strike, and at least one member of the NPC had argued for retaining the right to post big-character posters two years earlier.[9]

Chinese legal scholars have articulated with increasing force in recent years the view that the constitution is not merely a statement of past achievements and broad future aims, but must serve as a binding charter of citizens' rights and governmental powers and functions. For example, Wang Shuwen, director of the national Institute of Law of the Chinese Academy of the Social Sciences, contributed an article entitled "On the Supreme Legal Force of the Constitution" to a leading legal publication in 1981. Wang stated:

The direct binding force of the constitution is chiefly reflected in the following four aspects:

(1) The respective stipulations of the constitution are the direct legal basis for activity of all state organs and citizens. . . .

(2) The stipulations of the constitution possess direct legal binding force upon the activities of all state organs and citizens. . . .

(3) Whether or not there are similar provisions in pertinent legislation, constitutional stipulations with respect to the power and functions of state organs and the rights and duties of citizens constitute their original and direct source from the standpoint of their legal basis. . . .

(4) The various stipulations of the constitution are also the legal basis for all concrete actions taken by government organs. . . .

Some constitutional scholars deny or ignore the supreme legal force of the constitution as noted above. The reason for their view is that they believe that the various stipulations of the constitution are lacking concrete enforcement measures such as are found in the civil law, criminal law, and administrative law. It is true . . . the constitution cannot stipulate such concrete enforcement measures. . . . For just this reason, the stipulations of the constitution must be made more concrete and supplemented by ordinary laws. Nonetheless, one cannot take this as a reason for denying that the constitution has direct binding force. Otherwise, the result would be to rob of the requisite constitutional protection various constitutional provisions, such as the basic rights and freedoms of citizens.[10]

Another scholar, writing shortly before the promulgation of the 1982 constitution, agreed with the view that the constitution should be binding, but bemoaned the fact that all previous Chinese Communist constitutions had been ignored in practice by

Party and government officials. Though the problem of disregard for the constitution reached the extreme in the Cultural Revolution, it actually began in the 1950s, he observed. Calling upon the Party to adhere to the constitution and other laws, the author proposed establishment of a constitutional committee of nine to fifteen members, selected by the National People's Congress, to enforce the constitution.[11]

In the mid-1970s, many Chinese were dubious about the salience of constitutionally stipulated "citizens' rights."[12] But, by the late seventies, both respectable legal scholars and young political dissidents called upon the government strictly to honor the constitutional rights of citizens. Although the dissidents have been silenced through arrests of their leaders and suppression of unofficial journals, the trend toward greater reliance upon formal legality is likely to produce continued calls for progressive elaboration and legal protection of citizens' constitutional rights. This trend is affecting the evolution of concrete rules related to individual rights, as we will see in the following pages, although there remain certain ideological, conceptual, and systemic limits or conditions to enjoyment of the various freedoms of citizens prescribed in the constitution.

Most scholarly Chinese articles claim that human rights, or "citizens' rights" as they are usually called in Chinese documents, are in the main well protected by the state constitution and related laws.[13] Some articles, however, have openly declared that the struggle for human rights in China is not over yet. This view was forcefully expressed by the author of an article published in *Democracy and the Legal System* in 1980:

Some people, preparing to fix others, denounced 'human rights' as a 'bourgeois slogan.' . . . They did not know that the question of human rights had also been raised by the proletariat in the course of the revolution in China. . . . Some missions of the bourgeois democratic revolution, such as the realization of democracy, freedom, and human rights have not yet been fully realized. . . . There have never existed human rights in the abstract. . . . Human rights take the form of citizens' rights.[14]

Other articles strongly urge better legal protection of citizens' rights through more specific statutory stipulations and improved procedural safeguards, without explicitly invoking the language of international human rights.

It bears repeating that the Chinese constitution is prescriptive and prospective as well as descriptive and retrospective. It is not solely a statement of past achievements or a description of rights currently enjoyed by the Chinese citizen, although it does perform both of those functions. It expresses the intention that Chinese citizens "shall" enjoy certain rights, such as the right of men and women to equal pay for equal work (art. 48), that they do not necessarily enjoy yet.

Civil Rights in Chinese Law and Practice

Human rights are often divided into two broad categories—civil and political rights, and social, economic, and cultural rights. Both categories are discussed in what follows, but because political rights are treated in essay 3, they will be treated only incidentally here. It is convenient to compare the provisions of Chinese law, and practice thereunder, with the language and purport of comparable provisions of the pertinent international agreements. These are the Universal Declaration of Human Rights (UDHR), the International Covenant on Civil and Political Rights (ICCPR), and the International Covenant on Economic, Social, and Cultural Rights (ICESC).

The Chinese do not officially accept the application of these agreements on Chinese soil. Most Chinese writers on international law stress that the emergence of a growing body of rules on human rights within the corpus of modern international law does not confer rights directly upon individual human beings in China or any other country. Such rights must be created by appropriate domestic legislation. In short, Chinese scholars reject the notion that individuals can be subjects of international law with respect to human rights or any other purposes.[15] Moreover, any inquiry into the Chinese rights situation by a foreign government or international organization is regarded as intervention in Chinese domestic affairs and, consequently, a violation of international law. Thus, China has not adhered to the major international covenants on human rights—as the United States has not, but for different reasons.

On the other hand, the progressive elaboration of international human rights through successive treaties over the past three decades is now generally hailed by Chinese legal scholars as a positive development.[16] Soviet contributions to this progress are acknowledged, though most credit is given to the demands of the vast masses of peace-loving peoples of the Third World, whose rights were disregarded in the past. Chinese scholars and government spokesman often imply the validity of international human rights by condemning other countries for violating them.

In whatever way the Chinese view of international rights compacts evolves, they remain useful for organizing a discussion of rights law and practice in any country, including China. In the category of civil rights, the Universal Declaration (art. 3) and the International Covenant on Civil and Political Rights (arts. 6 and 9) declare that human beings have basic rights to life, liberty, security of person, and equality before the law. The two documents prohibit torture and slavery. They stipulate that everyone shall be free to leave any country, including his own, and grant the right to liberty of movement and to choose one's residence. They state that the individual shall enjoy freedom of conscience and religion, the right to hold opinions without interference, and the right to freedom of expression, subject to legal restriction to protect the rights or reputations of others, national security, or public health or morals. They prohibit arbitrary or unlawful interference with privacy, family, home, or correspondence. How is each of these rights treated in current Chinese law and practice?

Right to Life

Although no Chinese Communist constitution has contained an explicit provision guaranteeing the right to life, concern for human life is a strong traditional Chinese value that is deeply felt by citizens and reflected in Party and state policies. The swift, stern measures taken against murder and other forms of criminal violence toward another person demonstrate the strong social disapproval of violent invasion of personal rights. This concern is reflected also in the longstanding policy to use the death penalty sparingly and to avoid erroneously sentencing someone to die. As Chairman Mao once said, "Once a head is chopped off, history shows it can't be restored, nor can it grow again as chives do, after being cut."[17]

Despite great loss of life in wars and uprisings over the centuries, the Chinese have never taken the death of a human being lightly, whether it was caused by a wrongful act of another individual or resulted from a miscarriage of justice. In all eras, including the present, surviving relatives of a murdered or wrongfully executed person have borne a heavy moral obligation to see the wrong corrected and the death avenged. Whenever formal legal procedures have been ineffective, informal grievance mechanisms have arisen to provide review and remedy.

Today, ordinary citizens and state and Party leaders alike share the view that an aggrieved citizen should be able to obtain redress in the case of wrongful execution or other serious miscarriages of justice. Thus, in 1979 thousands of complainants bypassed local political, administrative, and legal organs, charging that they had proved ineffective, and flocked to Beijing to seek redress. After several months of delay and popular demonstrations, the Party and state leaders responded by sending special high-level investigators down to the localities to investigate. Many old decisions were overturned, and hundreds of thousands of erroneously convicted persons were exonerated—many posthumously—a perfect illustration of the nonfinality principle.

Chinese concern for human life does not extend to persons convicted of heinous crimes, including homicide and rape. China has no vocal group opposed to the dealth penalty, and, indeed, one hardly hears any opposition to it at all. "A life for a life" is generally regarded as both a fair punishment and an effective deterrent.

Right to Liberty

The right to individual liberty, central to Western political and legal thought, is explicitly declared in the UDHR (art.

3) and the ICCPR (arts. 6 and 9). In China constitutional prescriptions likewise recognize the citizen's right to liberty. All four PRC constitutions declare protection for "freedom of the person," in association with provisions barring arbitrary arrest and detention or illegal search. In the exercise of this freedom, or any other citizens' rights, however, the individual must not "infringe upon the interests of the state, of society, and of the collective, or upon the lawful freedoms and rights of other citizens" (art. 51 of the 1982 constitution). As Politburo member Peng Zhen said in his report on the draft state constitution, delivered to the Fifth Session of the Fifth National People's Congress on November 26, 1982:

In the history of the world there have never been any absolute rights and freedoms not subject to any limitations. We are a socialist country, in which the interests of the state and society are basically identical to the interests of the individual. Only when the democratic rights and basic interests of the vast masses of the people are guaranteed and developed will it be possible for the freedoms and rights of individual citizens to be completely guaranteed and fully realized.[18]

The millennial Chinese preference for public over private and others over self, reinforced by the current emphasis upon the socialist spiritual value of personal sacrifice for the collective interest, militates strongly against any tendency an individual might have to inflate into a charter of libertarianism the constitutional guarantee of freedom of the person. We should, of course, keep in mind that in the international documents, too, most individual rights are generally subject to limitation in deference to certain interests of society.

      Freedom of movement of the individual within China is restricted by the policy of banning any move from the place of registration except on assignment.[19] Since 1958, residents of rural areas have been able to relocate in urban areas only if they could obtain certification from the urban labor office that they possessed skills needed and unavailable in the city labor pool, a highly unlikely situation. A related freedom, choice of residence, present in the 1954 constitution, was omitted from subsequent constitutions. The policy underlying these restrictions on physical mobility is the need for controlled allocation of scarce commodities—space, jobs, housing, and food. As one Chinese commentator states:

Our new [1982 draft] constitution's stipulations concerning citizens' basic rights and freedoms are relatively realistic. . . . It provides guarantees where possible and where not possible it does not guarantee freedom (for example, it does not guarantee the freedom to change one's residence).[20]

Aside from limitations imposed by economic constraints, the Chinese citizen's constitutional right to freedom of the person has often been arbitrarily curtailed by unlawful acts of local Party and government officials. Although this type of encroachment on individual rights was most common during the Cultural Revolution, it has also occurred before and since. Now strongly disapproved by national policy, this kind of abuse is illustrated by a 1980 case in which a rural production brigade leader took the law into his own hands and beat up a commune member named He, detained him ten days, fined him 500 *yuan*, and confiscated some of his personal property because He stole a sheep. As reported in the nationally distributed Party newspaper, *People's Daily*, the story indicates that the brigade leader was arrested and punished for "encroaching upon He's freedom of the person and his inviolability of home."[21]

The Right to Equality Under the Law
Equality before the law is a fundamental tenet of the international human rights instruments, just as it was a fundamental political precept for the founding fathers of the United States. In the history of Chinese Communism, however, the concept of legal equality has had its ups and downs. Although the earliest extant Communist constitutional draft (1930) prescribed a policy of nondiscrimination and equality toward all working people, including peasants (art. 2), it called for the exercise of dictatorship over and suspension of all civil and political rights of warlords, bureaucrats, gentry, landlords, and exploitative capitalists (art. 6).
Other Chinese Communist constitutions, however, have contained provisions calling for "complete equality of all the peo-

ple" (Constitutional Document of the Shaan-Gan-Ning Border Region, April 23, 1946, chapter 2, art. 5),[22] or stating that "citizens of the PRC are equal before the law" (art. 85 of the 1954 constitution). The 1975 and 1978 constitutions, however, dispensed with any pretense of equality for all citizens.

Formal legal equality before the courts was restored by the "Organic Law for People's Courts," adopted on July 1, 1979; article 5 states that "the people's courts treat all citizens equally according to the law."[23] The principle of equality was restored to constitutional status by article 32 of the 1982 state constitution, which declares that "all citizens of the People's Republic of China are equal before the law." Women's rights to equal treatment have been accorded explicit recognition in each of the four PRC state constitutions.

Chinese legal scholars have differed over the meaning of the constitutional right of equality before the law. Some argue that it is restricted to equal procedural rights and that it would be absurd to accord equal political rights to opponents of socialism. Others maintain that all citizens should enjoy the same substantive as well as procedural rights.[24] Less debatable than the meaning of the constitutional term "equality" is the fact that the law is not always applied equally.[25] The Chinese press and legal journals frequently expose cases where persons with connections have avoided proper punishment through the use of influence.

Freedom of Thought, Conscience, and Religion
The International Covenant on Civil and Political Rights states that the individual shall enjoy freedom of thought, conscience, and religion (art. 18); the right to hold opinions without interference (art. 19.1); and the right to freedom of expression (art. 19.2), subject to legal restriction to protect the rights or reputation of others, national security, or public health or morals (art. 19.3). These freedoms are deemed fundamental to the development of any genuine individual personality or viable intellectual, artistic, and political expression. To what extent does Chinese law recognize and protect these rights and freedoms?

Despite the orthodoxy of the ideology of Marxism-Len-

inism—Mao Zedong Thought, current Chinese official policy con-
dones, but does not encourage, nonsocialist thought.[26] Rejecting
the Gang of Four's practice of punishing individuals for their private
beliefs, China's current criminal law punishes counterrevolutionary actions but not thoughts. The most expansive listing of people's
freedoms and rights, contained in the Common Programs of the
Northeastern and Inner Mongolian Regions (1946 and 1947, respectively), guaranteed freedom of thought.[27] However, none of
the four PRC state constitutions has explicitly endorsed freedom
of thought and conscience, though all have declared a freedom of
religious belief, as did the 1931 Chinese Soviet constitution (art.
13).[28]

Examination of the full record of Chinese Communist
constitutional documents, then, suggests that freedom of thought
has been consciously excluded from the roster of constitutionally
protected rights. This is hardly surprising, given the dominant role
of the Communist Party and the insistence that all citizens must
uphold the "four basic principles": socialism, Communist Party
leadership, Marxism-Leninism—Mao Zedong Thought, and the dictatorship of the proletariat.

Closely related to freedom of thought is freedom of
speech. Speech is the natural and logical extension of thought. Yet
it is also the bridge between thought and action, speech often
leading to behavior, both intended and unintended. As we know,
no society allows absolute freedom of speech. The oft-cited illustration of the absurdity of unlimited freedom of speech is that it
would permit someone falsely and maliciously to shout "fire" in
a crowded theater, causing mass panic leading to injury and death.
Speech per se is not made punishable by the PRC criminal code;
however, certain types of verbal or written expression have been
deemed crimes,[29] as several of the "Peking Spring" critics learned
the hard way. The rough rule of thumb seems to be that no speech
should run counter to the "four basic principles." Most important,
one may not oppose the leadership of the Communist Party or the
socialist system. Speech, as well as actions generally, must also
satisfy the rather broad requirements of articles 51, 52, 53, and
54 of the 1982 constitution which, respectively, require citizens

to refrain from infringing upon the interests of the state, society, and the collective, or upon the lawful rights and freedoms of other citizens; to safeguard the unity of the country; to protect state secrets; and to defend the security, honor, and interests of the motherland.[30]

One of the most dramatic demonstrations that the post-Mao liberalization represents a genuine relaxation of control in some areas is the increasing acceptability of public acts of religious devotion. Although all four PRC constitutions have declared that Chinese citizens "enjoy freedom of religious belief," the 1975 and 1978 versions revealed an official bias against religion by adding a phrase granting freedom "to propagate atheism," but not to promote religious belief; nominal balance has been restored by elimination of this provision in the 1982 constitution. While public religious services had all but disappeared by the late 1970s, by the early 1980s many churches, temples, and mosques had reopened; foreign visitors had observed young as well as older Chinese performing religious rituals such as burning incense sticks. Furthermore, young people are able to become monks, preachers, and priests. The only explicit legal constraint upon organized religion is that "no religious affairs may be dominated by any foreign country" (art. 36 of the 1982 constitution).

Right to Privacy and Freedom of Correspondence

An individual's right to privacy and to freedom of correspondence is protected by article 17 of the ICCPR. Likewise, all four PRC state constitutions have declared that "the freedom and privacy of correspondence of citizens . . . are protected by law" (art. 40 of 1982 constitution). This is not, however, an absolute right, as correspondence may be censored "to meet the needs of state security or of investigation into criminal offenses" (art. 40, 1982). Interviews with numerous former residents of China indicate very little govenmental interference with the domestic mails in ordinary times. The *People's Daily*, however, as recently as 1980, reported pressure by a local Party secretary to force local postal authorities to reveal records of phone calls, letters, and telegrams sent to central authorities by a critic of local party officials. The *People's Daily* editors sharply condemned this action by the local Party secretary, stating:

Every citizen has the legal right, protected by law, to reveal problems to higher levels of leading organs and the Party newspaper. No one may interfere with, block, or investigate such communications. . . . [Violation] cannot be tolerated by either Party discipline or state law. We trust the proper authorities will look into this matter and handle it.[31]

The story is interesting for two reasons. First, it suggests a genuine high-level concern for freedom of correspondence, at least where it concerns allegations of illegal activity. Second, rather than pursuing legal channels to vindicate the right to freedom of correspondence, the complainant wrote a letter to the *People's Daily*, whose editorial office, in essence, investigated and decided the case, and communicated the "precedent" throughout the entire country.

The official Party press, in the above case and many others, in effect performs a wide variety of legal functions: it acts as a finder of fact; "judges" the validity of claims; and acts in a quasi-legislative fashion by widely publicizing negative and positive "model cases," illustrating how or how not to construe new Party directives. It also helps to shape popular attitudes toward law through a continuing campaign of mass legal education. While the above related account illustrates how the press can help assure enjoyment of the constitutional right of free communication, this process of "law by press" also raises a host of other constitutional issues, such as the right to due process and the right of the accused Party official to legal protection of his good reputation (arts. 38 and 41).

House, Family, Honor, and Reputation
The international instruments prohibit "arbitrary interference with privacy, family, home, and correspondence," as well as attacks upon honor and reputation. These interests are all accorded constitutional recognition in China. Aside from freedom of

correspondence, which has been discussed already, all four PRC state constitutions have declared that the home is inviolable; the 1982 constitution added an article declaring the inviolability of the personal dignity of citizens and the prohibition of insult or slander in any form (art. 38). Interestingly, concern for personal reputation of innocent citizens was cited in 1980 as the chief justification for excising from the constitution the right to post big-character posters,[32] which had just earned headlines around the world as a result of the spontaneous outpouring of demands for democracy and reform popularly known as the "Peking Spring."[33]

Declaring that the home is inviolable does not, of course, make it so. Despite explicit constitutional mention, Chinese homes were entered at will, ransacked, and taken over illegally during the Cultural Revolution. In recent years, however, the government has adopted a policy of restoring homes to their original owners. Also, a restoration of police discipline has reportedly reduced illegal entry of homes by the authorities.

As for marriage and family, both are embraced by the constitutional provision that "the state protects marriage, the family, the mother, and child" (art. 49). Indeed, the PRC marriage law and criminal law both express a strong policy of protection of the marriage relationship, provided it is based on freedom of choice. Persons "interfering with marriage" are likely to be subjected to public criticism and administrative punishment and possibly even to criminal sanctions. Divorce is generally disfavored by public opinion and difficult in fact to obtain, despite a recent change in the marriage law to make it easier.[34] The not uncommon practice of assigning husbands and wives to jobs hundreds, if not thousands, of miles apart often puts an intolerable strain upon the Chinese marriage and family. Many couples see each other for only a week or so each year. Yet none is likely to demand a job near his or her spouse on the ground of the constitutional protection of the marriage. Such behavior would violate the dominant value of favoring collective over individual interests.

Another policy with serious impact upon the Chinese family is the birth-control program, sanctioned by articles 25 and

49 of the 1982 state constitution. In effect, couples may not have more than one child. Violators are subject to criticism and to discrimination in jobs, benefits, and children's educational opportunities. Some reports indicate that a mother becoming pregnant with a third child is forced, by her quasi-governmental neighborhood group, to undergo an abortion. Again, there are no reports of a challenge to these policies on constitutional grounds. News reports have suggested, however, that many peasants have successfully resisted the enforcement of family planning, because their income is dependent upon the number of workers in the family. Official state policy is to seek compliance through persuasion rather than force.

The Right to Physical Security
The right to security of the person against criminal violence by his fellow citizens is respected by jurisprudence of every organized society. In practice, however, nowhere can the right be fully enjoyed. Its protection is flawed by lack of police resources or by less than stringent enforcement measures. The social interest in order and security also usually competes with the right of the accused to due process of law. In China today the scales are weighted in favor of the protection of law-abiding citizens against violent criminal elements. The result is that, despite an acknowledged crime problem in the last decade, China's crime level is certainly well below that of Western countries.

But the human right to security does not mean simply the ability to walk home alone at night without the fear of being mugged. It also refers to individuals' rights to be secure from arbitrary restraint or from unlawful invasion of the home or the application of illegal coercion by the state. While all PRC state constitutions have declared the freedom of the person and the home to be inviolable and the 1982 constitution has added a provision declaring that the personal dignity of citizens is inviolable (art. 38), past practice has not lived up to this ideal. The Chinese press in recent years has been replete with articles exposing and condemning widespread rights violations involving unlawful arrest, execution of the innocent, and even the use of torture.

Procedural Rights

Violations of fundamental citizens' rights in China have often been attributed to the past weakness of the legal system. Thus, it is not surprising that one of the first fruits of the current legal reform movement was the promulgation of codes of criminal law and procedure.[35] These measures helped to bring Chinese constitutional and legal requirements closer to the international instruments model of due process. Thus, the UDHR and the ICCPR prohibit arbitrary arrests, mandate equality before the law, and establish strict standards of due process for the defendant in criminal proceedings—including equality before the courts, the presumption of innocence, prompt and effective notice of charges against him, choice of counsel, prompt trial, the right to defense, the right to examine witnesses against him, and the right not to testify against himself or to confess guilt.

The Chinese constitution, code of criminal procedure, and other laws provide for a number of the procedural rights enumerated by the international instruments. These include independence of the judiciary, public trial in most cases, rights to a defense and to an appeal, and protection against arbitrary arrest and detention.

Past encroachments upon the physical liberties of the Chinese citizen, despite a strong policy forbidding such behavior, have been officially linked to inadequate procedural protections. Efforts to remedy the situation have led to a more rigorous arrest and detention law and to a criminal procedure code that imposes stricter limits on police and prosecutorial action. Confessions are no longer required for conviction, and independent corroborating evidence is necessary for conviction when a confession has been obtained.[36] Independence of the judiciary "according to law" has been restored by the 1982 constitution (art. 126). Citizens are also accorded a constitutional right to appeal any transgression of law or neglect of duty by any state authority and to secure compensation "in accordance with the law" for loss suffered through infringement of their rights as citizens (art. 41).

Despite these marked improvements in constitutional and statutory provisions relating to protection of individuals accused or convicted of crimes, it seems that practice lags behind the ideals of the new laws. For example, Western reporters have charged that the "Peking Spring" dissidents were imprisoned as a result of a show trial (in the case of Wei Jingsheng), no trial at all, or through arbitrary administrative proceedings leading to labor reeducation.[37] In addition, there have even been official departures from the standards of the new criminal code. For example, the various deadlines and procedural formalities of the new code were waived if the alleged crime occurred prior to the date the code became law. This policy was justified on the basis of a lack of judges and lawyers. The urgent need to "maintain order and stability and strike hard at criminal elements" required employment of the simpler summary measures of the past. Although it might be argued in defense of this measure that genuine criminal elements could not complain because the law applied was the one in force at the time of the offense, this logic would hardly be compelling in the case of one innocent of the crime charged.

Another measure reflecting the Chinese government's preference for social order over procedural concerns was the suspension of the criminal procedure code's requirements that the Supreme People's Court review all death penalties. In June 1981, the Standing Committee of the National People's Congress issued a decision authorizing carrying out the death penalty, in all cases except those involving counter revolution and corruption, simply upon a single review by an intermediate People's Court. The justification was the need to set a stern and swift example for other criminal elements.[38] The execution in August 1982 of five would-be plane hijackers, four weeks after their aborted effort, demonstrates how swiftly criminal retribution can operate in China.[39] Foreign press reports of the thousands of death penalties announced in China between July and November 1983 declare that in some cases execution took place scarcely more than a week after the crime—sometimes without public trial and without higher court review.[40]

Despite China's recent adoption of more extensive constitutional and statutory stipulations protective of individual rights, it would be misleading to equate Chinese procedural rules, not to mention current practice, with the essentially Western due process model set forth in the international instruments. While the ICCPR clearly envisages an adversarial procedure designed to provide utmost protection to a defendant presumed to be innocent, prevailing Chinese policy stresses the paramount interests of society, the state, and socialist modernization. There is no presumption of innocence (though some Chinese academicians have apparently argued for its adoption),[41] and no right to counsel prior to trial. As for the defense counsel, instead of being a vigorous independent advocate of his client's innocence, he is a state employee committed to help the prosecutor and the judge fight crime.

The preferred nonadversarial, nonjudicial mode of conflict resolution in the PRC pervasively shapes the fate of human rights in China, however close the language of the Chinese constitutional provision may be to its counterpart in the international instruments. No matter how unambiguous the promised right or freedom may be, it is not expected that the citizen will use the formal legal mechanisms to secure its enjoyment. As suggested above, whenever two Chinese private citizens quarrel, the probable means of solution is through mediation by a respected third party or conciliation by leaders of the units with which the disputants are affiliated.

Where the state is a party to the dispute, the citizen faces a triple barrier. First, his rights and interests may pale when weighed, as they are required to be, against the interests of the state and society. Second, the state, as the source of the citizen's right, defines the content of that right in a particular situation. Third, the main channels of complaint and redress at the local level are likely to be controlled by the state or Party official who has allegedly infringed upon the citizen's rights. Lacking well-developed legal procedures for rights enforcement and finding local administrative channels blocked, the citizen often must swallow his grievance or resort to the time-honored channels of "letters and visits" to higher levels of the Party and state bureaucracy.[42]

The right to make such appeals first emerged during the imperial era in the form of "capital appeals" in Peking, initiated by banging a drum outside the palace of the emperor. If the complainant's charge was vindicated, he preserved his right and reputation. If it was not vindicated, he would lose his liberty and possibly his life, as well as endanger his entire family. Yet many people took that chance because of a firmly held conviction that they had suffered injustice and that redress could be obtained if they could only find an honest official, even if it meant going all the way to the top.

The persistence of the traditional right of recourse up the administrative ladder is reflected in the PRC constitutional provision that citizens may complain to government officials about infringement of their rights. It may be significant, however, that the phrase "organs of state at any level," present in the 1978 constitution (art. 55), is replaced in 1982 by "relevant organs of state" (art. 40). It may well be that China's current leaders think regular process at the local level should be made more accessible and competent so that high-level nonjudicial Party and state officials are not called upon to substitute their judgment for that of the court. This interpretation draws support from the effort to train more judicial personnel, as well as lawyers and prosecutors, and to end the practice of local Party secretaries reviewing and revising judicial decisions. Despite the apparent sincerity of the pledge of China's leaders to leave adjudication to courts "independent under the law," the pervasive role of the Party in approving and reviewing criminal sentences will take time to dismantle. For even the work of "restoring socialist legality" and correcting hundreds of thousands of misjudged cases after 1977 was handled largely by Party organs instead of the judiciary.

Another area of punishment not subject to the full panoply of due process protection of the Chinese constitution is the "re-education through labor" sanction administered to repeating minor offenders and political dissidents not charged with felonies.[43] Assigned by a committee of police, labor, and personnel officials to hard labor in camps for periods of up to three years, persons subject to "education" are not entitled to public trial or legal counsel. In theory they do not need any such protections because they are being "educated" and not "punished."

Economic, Social, and Cultural Rights

Not surprisingly, Chinese government spokesmen and legal scholars generally endorse the common socialist position that economic, social, and cultural rights are at least as important as political and civil rights. Indeed, Chinese commentators invariably stress that without the material and legal guarantee of the enjoyment by all citizens of basic economic, social, and cultural rights, there can be no genuine enjoyment of political and civil rights.[44]

As for economic rights of Chinese citizens, while claiming that the vast majority of the people in socialist China are better off than workers in capitalist societies, the Chinese authorities in recent years have acknowledged that present reality falls far short of the communist ideal of abundance. Practical constraints are acknowledged, for example, in several articles of the new constitution which provide that the state will take measures to create the material conditions necessary to make it possible for citizens to enjoy fully their economic, social, and cultural rights.[45] Chinese constitutional guarantees of the economic, social, and cultural rights of citizens cover every major category contained in the International Covenant on Economic, Social, and Cultural Rights. The degree of correspondence between the Chinese and the ICESC differs, however, from category to category. Moreover, there has been fluctuation over time from one Chinese constitution to another, not to mention the gap between the legal ideal and social practice.

Right to Work and Minimum Conditions of Employment

Article 11 of the ICESC sets forth the right to enjoy an "adequate standard of living." While the state is obliged to help those who cannot help themselves, the principal assurance of an adequate standard of living is through realization of a basic right to work (art. 6). This right is not satisfied by the simple provision of any job; in addition, the individual must have freedom to choose his employment (art. 6). The ICESC articulates additional requirements relating to the work relationship, nature of compensation, and condition of the working place. Thus, workers should be granted the right to form unions (art. 8); equal pay for equal work (art. 7)—with particular emphasis on equal treatment of women; the right to rest (art. 7d); and the right to safe and healthy working conditions (art. 7).

Given the Marxist tenet that labor is the true source of value, it is natural that the Chinese Communist Party from the beginning showed particular concern for workers' rights. While the Chinese Soviet constitution of 1931 did not explicitly declare a right to work, it did stipulate a number of workers' rights that foreshadowed several provisions of the 1966 ICESC. For example, article 5 grants to the workers the right to supervise production, to enjoy an eight-hour day, and to receive a minimum wage.[46]

The four PRC constitutions have all proclaimed that citizens have a right to work, but none has extended this to imply a right to choose the place and type of work. On the contrary, the several PRC state constitutions have each indicated that the citizen has a duty to work at the job to which he is assigned by the state. The 1982 constitution explicitly pairs the obligation with the right (art. 42), while earlier versions noted that "work is an honorable duty for every citizen able to work" (art. 10 of the 1978 constitution), or "work is a matter of honor for every citizen . . . able to work" (art. 16 of the 1954 constitution). The most radical of the PRC constitutions, that of 1975, stated the linkage most bluntly with the phrase "He who does not work, neither shall he eat" (art. 9). This principle no longer represents either Chinese law or Chinese policy. Thus, an article in *Fazhi bao* (Legal System News) in September 1980 stated that all citizens, even counterrevolutionaries, have the right to receive clothing and food.[47] One prominent Chinese legal scholar criticized the principle of "no work—no eat" as unreasonable and unrealistic at a time when the state was unable to guarantee employment for everyone seeking work.[48]

In practice, Chinese governmental authorities have enforced the linkage principle in connection with the right and duty to work. Thus, the *People's Daily* in June 1982 reported that the Beijing Municipal Bureau of Higher Education had deprived four college graduates of their right to job placement because they refused to accept jobs assigned to them by the state.[49]

The Chinese citizen's lack of freedom to choose his job should be considered in the light of two important circumstances. First, the Chinese government in recent years has acknowledged considerable unemployment, particularly among teenagers, a problem China shares with many other countries. Thus, the 1982 state constitution implicitly recognizes the shortage of suitable work: "The state creates conditions for employment through various channels and, on the basis of increased production, gradually improves working conditions, strengthens labor protection, and raises remuneration for work" (art. 42). Second, higher education in China is largely subsidized by the state, so that requiring graduates to conform to the "unified assignment" system can be justified on quasi-contractual grounds.

With respect to the work relationship, while unions have been restored in state enterprises, and workers' and staff congresses have been established to play a role in policy-making and supervision,[50] Chinese workers do not have a constitutional right to an equal bargaining position vis-à-vis their employer—the state or the collective. On the contrary, the Chinese worker is duty-bound to obey enterprise rules and follow the directions of management. The individual worker does not have a viable option to quit and seek another comparable job. Nor is the union supposed to promote workers' economic interests through confrontation with the employer. The ultimate weapon of organized labor, the strike, is not available. Although the first draft Chinese Soviet constitution (1930) and the radical 1975 and 1978 constitutions both prescribed a right to strike, it was intended for use against mistaken policies or bureaucratic mismanagement, not to secure higher wages. The right to strike was eliminated from the 1982 constitution as a potentially destabilizing mechanism.[51]

As for the ICESC's standards regarding compensation, the last three PRC constitutions all set forth the basic principle of "from each according to his ability, to each according to his work" (art. 6 of the 1982 constitution; art. 9 of 1975; art. 10 of 1978).

Explicit attention is given by Chinese constitutions, as by the ICESC, to the issue of equal pay for men and women. Thus, in the 1954 and 1975 versions, it is stated that women "enjoy equal rights with men in all spheres" (arts. 96 and 27, respectively). In 1978, to the above general statement is added the specific clarification "Men and women enjoy equal pay for equal work" (art. 53). The 1982 constitution contains a similar provision stating that "the state guarantees the rights and interests of women, and implements the principle of equal pay for men and women who do equal work" (art. 48). Another interesting feature related to this issue is that during the process of public debate and revision of the 1982 draft constitution, a phrase was added to this clause stating that the state "trains and appoints women as government cadres." The addition appears to imply recognition that an insufficient number of women are appointed to government offices and a resolution to improve the situation. The new clause does not, however, adopt a standard of nondiscrimination or numerical equality in such appointments.

Right to Social Security

What rights does a human being have when he can find no job or is too infirm or old to earn a living? In short, when the right to work fails to provide a reliable guarantee of the "adequate standard of living" provided by article 11 of the ICESC, what other human right can the individual fall back on? The answer given by the ICESC is that the state is obligated to assure enjoyment of the human right to "social security" (art. 9). How closely does the Chinese constitutional model conform to the international standard, and how well does Chinese practice adhere to the constitutional declarations and guarantees?

Beginning in 1931, Chinese Communist constitutions have uniformly recognized a right to "social insurance and unemployment pay"[52] or to "material assistance from the state and society in old age, illness, or disability" (1982 constitution, art. 45). While this right was limited to the working class in earlier constitutions, in the 1982 version it is extended to all citizens. But is this merely a hope, a statement of current reality, or something in between—a minimum guarantee with a promise of expansion as the national economy grows? To help answer this question, we should examine an additional statement in article 45 (1982): "To ensure that citizens can enjoy their right, the state expands social insurance, social assistance, and public health services." The implication is clear—present enjoyment cannot be complete; nor does the citizen have a constitutional right to complain, for he is on notice that the right is a limited one that will expand along with the state's capabilities.

Simply reading the constitution does not convey the full picture of current social security, welfare, and public health rights. The fact is that while employees of state enterprises and their dependents do enjoy protection in all three areas, workers in collective enterprises or in agricultural pursuits (more than 80 percent of the population) receive virtually no coverage from the state. Most of the benefits they do receive—meager compared to state employees—are provided by their children or by the collective unit to which they belong.[53] The agricultural production team (or villager's small group) guarantees a basic grain ration for each family. Limited health services are available in some places for a small fee at cooperative facilities at the brigade (village) and commune (township) level.

Because the constitution adopts the principle of "to each according to his labor," in the absence of uniform state subsidies there are wide variations in individual and family incomes, though far from as glaring as the inequalities present in the old days. State welfare funds and supplies are made available in emergencies when the resources of family, community, and collective organization do not suffice.

Right to Education

The 1931 Chinese Soviet constitution anticipated the ICESC (art. 13) in yet another respect by declaring that all workers, peasants, and laboring masses had the right to receive free education (art. 12).[54] Given the state of civil war prevailing at the time and the short life of the Jiangxi Soviet (three years), it is unlikely that this right could have been fully implemented. The principle of a right to free education was perpetuated by the 1946 Constitutional Principles of the Shaan-Gan-Ning Border Region (art. 3).[55] After the Communist Party gained national power, however, its leaders apparently realized the enormous cost of a nationwide system of free public education. As a result, although the four post-1949 constitutions have all declared that Chinese citizens have the right to education, none has contained an explicit undertaking by the state to provide all education free of charge. Education in China is not just a right; it is also a duty. Thus, the 1982 constitution pairs the right with an obligation to receive an education (art. 46).

In practice, education through elementary school in China is almost universal; although quite inexpensive, it is not completely free. After elementary school, the percentage of the population attending school declines markedly, particularly in rural areas. This is due to a combination of scarcity of trained teachers and the demand for teenagers to participate in family productive activities. Higher education is free, but available to no more than three percent of the college-age population.[56] Admission to college is now by competitive uniform national exam, largely replacing the political criteria of the Cultural Revolution.

Property Rights

Chinese authors attack the UDHR provision classifying the right to own private property as a protected human right.[57] This does not seem surprising in view of China's Marxist ideology and claim to have basically eliminated the private ownership of the means of production by 1956.

Yet it would be misleading to conclude that China has completely eliminated private, or individual, property from either its roster of constitutional rights or from economic or social reality. For in fact, China not only protects socialist collective and state-owned property; the successive PRC state constitutions have all contained provisions protecting the citizen's right to "ownership of legal income, savings, houses, and other legal property" (art. 13 of 1982; art. 9 of 1978; arts. 8–11 of 1954). In addition, the 1982 constitution (art. 13) restores the citizen's right to inherit private property present in the 1954 constitution (art. 12) but dropped in the 1975 and 1978 versions.

Even capitalist ownership of the means of production was accorded explicit constitutional protection by the 1954 constitution, though not by its successors. In a limited sense, however, capitalist property rights were restored in 1982 to constitutional protection by the provision (art. 18) granting foreign corporations, organizations, and individuals permission to invest in China and providing protection to their legal rights and interests.

Skeptics again may argue that these constitutional protections of individual property rights are window dressing, concocted to enhance China's image as a legitimate state replete with all the trappings of socialist legality. Anyone familiar with the horror stories published in China about the violation of citizens' rights during the Cultural Revolution would not be surprised to hear that this "ultraleft" convulsion had completely obliterated all property rights. Although destruction of valuable books and artifacts did occur, particularly where the owner was a former capitalist or bourgeois intellectual, the remarkable fact is that private property rights—for example, rights with respect to houses and bank accounts—have been generally well-respected by the authorities. In fact, until quite recently the Chinese government has generally shown such extreme deference toward urban homeowners that the authorities have abandoned plans to widen streets or erect modern apartments, declining to invoke the constitutional power of eminent domain against stubborn householders. Moreover, houses illegally commandeered by Party officials during the Cultural Revolution are supposed to be returned to their original owners, though enforcement of the policy has been sluggish.

The reason why private property not involving means of production has fared relatively well is that the constitutional right to personal property, the ideology of Marxism-Leninism–Mao Zedong Thought, and pragmatic politics are all in harmony. In theory, personal property will remain even after Communism is attained. Moreover, recognition of a right to security of ownership and use of property, and to transmission of property to one's descendants, is a powerful means of eliciting maximum productivity. Given the shift in Party policy since December 1978 from political struggle to economic development, it is likely that the economic rights of individuals and other entities will receive increasingly explicit legal protection.

Prospects for Human Rights in China

The prospects for human rights in any society are a function of the interaction of a number of factors: popular values and aspirations; the prevailing political-legal ideology, structure, and trends; and various "objective" forces, including domestic economic circumstances and the influence of foreign models and the international human rights movement. Projection of probable trends in the prescription and implementation of human rights in China naturally must begin with an understanding of the present situation and an analysis of the conceptual, institutional, and material factors that have shaped the current form of rights in China today.

We have noted that Chinese citizens are promised— by the state constitution and other laws—a number of the rights set forth in the "international bill of rights." Enjoyment of these rights, while generally denied to certain individuals on political grounds (for example, opposition to the socialist system) or denied to almost everyone in periods such as the Cultural Revolution, has basically improved over time. The scope and vigor of individual rights in China at any given moment is largely dependent upon the will of a small group of top Party leaders. This reflects both the influence of tradition and the Soviet model of a highly centralized political system.

Certain values that have been accorded unique emphasis in Chinese thought, as well as in China's social and political practice, have continuing salience today. Among these are a deeply held belief in an innate human right to life and to a just result in a legal proceeding. These conceptions have constantly reemerged in Chinese substantive law and judicial process. In other areas of civil, political, economic, social, and cultural rights, the scope of expectations to which the average Chinese citizen feels entitled has expanded in an evolutionary fashion with the increasing complexity and prosperity of society.

The array of rights of PRC citizens also reflects the influence of rights first originated in other countries or articulated in the international instruments. Some of these claims, such as the right to work, can be viewed as having "trickled down" into the consciousness of ordinary Chinese. Unemployed Chinese believe they have a right to work, and no Party or government official would disagree with them. Though no citizen would think to sue the government for a job, the Party and government clearly feel a strong obligation to increase employment opportunities, even if it means a limited restoration of private ownership of small enterprises.

Despite elimination of some rights from the new constitution, such as the right to strike, and despite renewed emphasis on the Communist ethic of self-denying service to society and the current stress on adherence to the "four basic principles" and other citizens' duties, certain other developments suggest that the individual rights situation in China may yet develop in the direction of the model established in the international instruments. The commitment to an increasingly formal model of domestic legality, together with China's growing involvement in international legal activities, are conducive to an expansion of the individual rights of Chinese citizens. Given China's long-established humanistic values and deeply held expectations of fair government, it is hoped that individual rights will grow as the economy develops and the country's leaders become increasingly committed to the rule of law at home and in the international arena.

3.

Political Rights
in Chinese Constitutions

Andrew J. Nathan

*P*olitical rights occupy a special place among human
rights. One can debate whether they are the most
fundamental, or whether social and economic welfare rights are
in some sense prior.[1] But in any case a special role must be con-
ceded to them. They are the means by which the citizen can, if
at all, pursue and protect his or her other rights. They provide
access to the political arena where substantive claims and conflicts
of interest are ultimately resolved. Also, everyone agrees that political rights are a crucial element of democracy, however that
disputed term might be further defined. In socialist states, the of-

In addition to the acknowledgments in the preface, I wish to thank the John Simon Gug-
genheim Memorial Foundation as well as the Joint Committee on Contemporary China of
the Social Science Research Council and the American Council of Learned Societies for
financial support that contributed to the writing of my chapters in this book. In writing both
chapters, I received valuable criticisms from Thomas P. Bernstein, Chang P'eng-yuan, Chou
Yang-shan, Gong Xiangrui, Steven I. Levine, and Roxane Witke; from Irene Bloom, Wm.
Theodore deBary, and other members of the Columbia University Seminar on Neo-Confucianism; and from Guy Alitto, Leo Ou-fan Lee, Tang Tsou, and other participants in a
seminar at the University of Chicago.

ficial philosophy identifies democracy chiefly with the pursuit of the people's higher interests, rather than with their ability to influence government. But these states also accept that the people's rights to supervise the bureaucracy and to participate in overseeing the organs of state are important elements of democracy.

In this essay I define political rights broadly as rights to act to influence the choice of government personnel or policy. I include the rights to vote, serve in office, petition, and appeal, as well as some of the rights often called civil rights, such as those to speak, publish, assemble, and associate. I also discuss other rights that have appeared in Chinese constitutions and which bear on political action. Table 1 lists the rights included in the discussion and shows how they have been treated in eleven constitutions and major constitutional drafts from the late Qing period to the most recent charter of the People's Republic.

In trying to analyze the meaning of political rights in China and to assess their vitality in practice, I am not imposing a foreign preoccupation. Rights are an issue that modern Chinese have placed in the forefront of their own concerns. Chinese thinkers have accepted the concept of rights for almost a century, not just out of deference to international trends but for strong reasons of their own. Political rights in particular have been stressed at each stage of reform and revolution in the twentieth century. They have been included in all Chinese constitutions, elaborated and emphasized more than in many Western constitutions.

Constitutions are a good starting place for the study of rights because they represent the negotiated consensus of at least some dominant groups in a society on basic political questions. They are written with self-conscious care and use legal and philosophical terms with some precision. Even their ambiguities have a purpose. Properly interpreted, constitutions tell us much about "what a society pretends or aspires to [and] where individual rights stand in its political system and scale of values."[2] Moreover, if a society has had a series of constitutions, especially under changing regimes, then much can be learned from the changes and continuities among them. The ideas that survive from constitution to constitution, that are shared by competing groups, and that are appealed to even by politicians who otherwise behave unconstitutionally form a constitutional tradition of basic, widely held values and so offer insight into an important part of a nation's political culture. The Chinese constitutional tradition so far as it concerns political rights forms the focus of this essay.

Throughout the essay the reader will find comparisons with the conception of rights in the United States. Occasionally the comparison is explicit. Often it is implicit in my choice of aspects of the Chinese tradition to highlight. In selecting American values as the main point of comparison, I do not mean to suggest that they embody universal standards against which all other countries should be measured. Rather, I compare the two systems because they display a challenging combination of broad rhetorical similarities with deep differences in values and practices. Only through careful comparison can the differences be seen for what they are—real and profound, not just shadings of interpretation. This done, not everyone will agree on which system is better, or that either is. But at least the comparison will be real. The statement, for example, that rights are not absolute in either system will not be the end of discussion, as it often too glibly is. One will be able to ask to what degree rights are limited, by what processes, and for what purposes, and how the limits are allowed to be challenged. Moreover, as argued in the preface, there are important ways in which the comparison between Chinese and American rights systems has application beyond the two countries themselves. Each is prominent in a group of nations holding roughly similar values, the socialist and the pluralist, liberal-democratic states, respectively. To be sure, America is unusual even among Western nations for the strength of the antithesis its rights ideology draws between the interests of the individual and those of the state, while China's version of socialist rights ideology has many features special to itself. Nor is the socialist/pluralist antithesis absolute. China and Japan, for example, share Confucian traditions, though winnowing and adapting them to different ends; America today protects as many welfare rights as political rights—more than many socialist states. Yet in the end China and other socialist states do often differ from the United States and other liberal-democratic

Table 1. Political Rights in Chinese Constitutions

Right or Freedom	Principles	Provisional Constitution	Temple Draft	1923	1931 (Tutelage)	1946	Jiangxi Program	1954	1975	1978	1982
Speech	X	X	X	X	X	X	X	X	X	X	X
Writing	X	X	X	X	implicit	X	O	see Freedom of culture	O	see Freedom of culture	see Freedom of culture
Publishing	X	X	X	X	X	X	X	X	X	X	X
Assembly/Association	X	X	X	X	X	X	X	X	X	X	X
Teaching/Study	O	O	O	O	O	X	O	O	O	O	O
Petition/Appeal/Suit	X	X	X	X	X	X	O	X	X	X	X
Compensation	O	O	O	O	O	X	O	X	O	O	X
Secrecy of correspondence	O	X	X	X	X	X	O	X	"freedom of"	"freedom of"	X
Equality before law	O	X	X	X	X	X	working classes	X	O	O	X
Popular Sovereignty	O	X	implicit	X	X	X	working classes	X	X	X	X
Voting	implicit	X	X	X	locally	X	working classes	X	"democratic consultion"	X	X
Running for office	implicit	X	X	X	O	X	working classes	X	X	X	X

Rights	1	2	3	4	5	6	7	8	9	10	11	12
Serving in office/sitting for exam	X	O	X	O	X	X locally	X	O	O	O	O	O
Election/Recall/Initiative/Referendum	O	O	O	O	O	O	election + recall	election + recall	election + recall in capitalist enterprises	election + recall	election + recall implicit	election + recall
Residual freedoms/rights	O	O	O	O	X	O	O	X	O	O	O	O
Supervision of production	O	O	O	O	O	O	X	X	O	O	O	X
Participation in armed revolution	O	O	O	O	O	O	working classes	O	O	O	O	O
National minority self-determination	O	O	O	O	O	O	X	O	O	O	O	O
National minority autonomy	O	O	O	O	O	O	X	X	X	X	X	X
Political asylum	O	O	O	O	O	O	X	X	X	X	X	X
Rights for foreign nationals	O	O	O	O	O	O	working classes	O	O	O	O	O
Procession/Demonstration	O	O	O	O	O	O	O	O	X	X	X	X
Freedom of culture: scientific research, literary and artistic creation, other cultural activities	see writing	see writing	see writing	see writing	see writing	see writing	O	O	O	O	O	O
Supervision of state organs	O	O	O	O	O	O	O	X	X	O	X	X
"Four greats"	O	O	O	O	O	O	O	O	O	X	X	O
Striking	O	O	O	O	O	O	O	O	O	X	X	O

KEY

X: The constitution confers this right, although perhaps not in exactly these words.

O: The constitution does not confer this right.

Details are contained in the appropriate sections of the text.

states on rights issues. A careful comparison of Chinese and American rights values should thus help clarify some internationally important issues.

If the Sino-U.S. comparison is useful for intellectual reasons, it is also important for policy reasons. As Westerners, we need to be reminded that the meaning of rights is contested, that alternative conceptions are not merely "immature" but have strong roots both in other cultures and in theories adapted from the West, and that the values at stake are important. Chinese spokesmen invite comparison of "bourgeois" and "socialist" human rights, arguing that only in the socialist systems are rights extensively enjoyed, broad in scope, and fully implemented.[3] These claims should be soberly evaluated, not polemically but through careful analysis of what the various rights systems lead to in theory and practice. Whatever dialogue the West may undertake with Chinese on rights issues will be more effective for being more realistic. The limited areas where values are similar are good places to seek agreement. The large areas where values diverge will doubtless be discussed and explored—and argued over—for decades. Of course, neither society is unanimous in its approach to rights. Some groups in each society are sympathetic to aspects of the dominant tradition in the other. This may also provide opportunities for mutual influence.

China has had twelve officially promulgated central government constitutions and numerous constitutional drafts since 1908.[4] Nine constitutions and two drafts—a total of eleven texts— are generally recognized as most important. I will trace the evolution of political rights through the eleven texts, with passing reference to other texts as well. I will trace which rights were added and subtracted, how the philosophical and legal status of rights and of the persons who held them developed, and how rights were interpreted in legislation, court action, and philosophical and legal commentary. Since the major purpose of political rights is to enable citizens to influence government, I will also describe each constitution's conception (if any) of popular sovereignty and the arrangements it provided for the people to exercise their sovereignty. Finally, political rights in any society are affected by arrangements for interpretation and enforcement of the constitution. In the United States, for example, the doctrine of judicial review has proven crucial for protecting rights. I will describe where each Chinese constitution placed the power to interpret rights.

Rights in constitutions are not coterminous with rights in practice. Some of the most oppressive political systems in history have been founded on beautiful-sounding and well-argued theories of rights. Some of the societies where rights are most vital lack clear constitutional or legal theories to support them. In England rights are established mainly by the force of legal tradition and public opinion. Rights were mentioned only in passing in the French constitution of 1958, but were well articulated in other widely accepted political and legal writings.[5] In the American constitution rights were an afterthought. Similarly, the institutions that defend rights—courts, procuracies, legislatures, private associations, political parties, trade unions—may be elaborately described in a constitution but weak in practice, or may be vigorous without clear constitutional sanction, as in the case of political parties and judicial review in the United States. Still further, the accepted content of a given right changes in response to political pressures and tides of public belief. The meaning of equal protection of the law, for example, has expanded vastly in recent decades in the United States.[6] Judges, politicians, and the public decide what a particular right means in a particular case, and say when it has to give way to an overriding social interest. Constitutions may or may not accommodate such legal and political developments either in prospect, leaving room for rights to evolve or be restricted in the future, or in retrospect, incorporating changes through amendment or revision. In short, the task of identifying a constitutional tradition involves not just an understanding of what successive constitutions said and were thought to say, but also an appreciation of how political forces have affected constitutional practice. Our focus must therefore be on the Chinese constitutions in their full intellectual and political contexts. Constitutions are a window on the rights system as a whole.

The eleven constitutional texts represent the thinking of four very different regimes—the last imperial dynasty, the liberal republic, the authoritarian Guomindang government, and the socialist People's Republic. This makes all the more striking certain continuities in the conception of political rights from one constitution to the next, which it will be the aim of this chapter to identify. Exploring the major values and ideas that help to explain these continuities will be the task of chapter 4.

The Early Constitutions

China's first constitutional draft was the Principles of the Constitution (Qinding xianfa dagang), published by the imperial government on August 27, 1908.[7] It was not a full constitution but a twenty-three article précis of principles to be put into effect toward the end of a nine-year reform period. The Qing dynasty had launched an ambitious program to modernize education, finance, the military, and government, with the full-scale constitution to be promulgated in 1916. The purpose of the Principles, like that of the entire reform program, was to strengthen the state and preserve the powers of the emperor. As the Empress Dowager put it in the edict that launched the constitution-drafting process in 1906: "The wealth and strength of other countries are due to their practice of constitutional government, in which public questions are determined by consultation with the people. The ruler and his people are as one body animated by one spirit."[8]

The Principles consisted of two parts, a fourteen-item list of the powers of the monarch and a nine-item appendix containing the rights and duties of subjects. Of the nine items in the appendix, three concerned political rights.

> [1.] Those subjects who have the qualifications fixed by laws or commands may be chosen to serve as civil or military officials or members of parliament.
> [2.] Within the scope of the law, subjects are granted the freedom of speech, writing, publication, and assembly and association. . . .
> [4.] Subjects can request judicial officials to judge matters that they petition to bring before them.

The Outline Electoral Law published with the constitutional principles hinted at an additional right to vote and to stand for elective office. It stated that "those who lack the legal qualifications shall not vote or stand for office." By implication, those not so disqualified had these rights. However terse, this initial package of political rights contained the fundamental elements for political participation.

But the Principles' grants were not really "rights" as that term is understood in the West. First, they were the emperor's gift. The document itself was *qinding*—imperially granted. The section on subjects' rights and duties was not coordinate with that on the emperor's powers but was an appendix. The rights were not granted to "citizens" (*guomin* or *gongmin*) or "the people" (*renmin*) as in later constitutions, although these terms were known. Instead the term *chenmin*, subjects, was used. Second, instead of limiting the scope of subsequent law, the rights sketched in the Principles were to be shaped and restricted by future laws. The law-making power was reserved to the emperor, drawing upon the nonbinding advice and recommendations of parliament. Two laws already existed which indicated how rights might have fared if the constitutional monarchy had come to pass. The 1907 Regulations on Association and Assembly said that any associations "whose goals are improper, or which contravene regulations, or stir up incidents, or harm public morals are to be carefully investigated by local officials and dissolved if their crime is light, punished if it is heavy."[9] The 1906 police regulations on newspapers forbade "slandering the Court, inappropriately discussing government affairs, obstructing peace and order, damaging public morals, publishing information on foreign or domestic affairs which has been designated secret by the relevant offices," and so on.[10] These regulations relied heavily on the discretion of enforcing officials to determine the boundaries of permissible acts. Rights defined by laws of this type had no independent content except that given by administrative interpretation.

Two documents published along with the Principles outlined the role of the future parliament and the methods of its election.[11] Unlike later constitutions the Principles contained no promise of popular sovereignty. The emperor was sovereign and parliament advisory. The parliament that was convened in 1910 consisted of 100 members appointed by the emperor and 100 elected by the provincial assemblies, themselves indirectly elected in 1909 by electoral colleges chosen, in turn, by a "silk-gown" franchise consisting of no more than half a percent of the population, all male.[12] Thus the political influence of the people was heavily buffered. The Principles of the Constitution reserved to the emperor the power to appoint judges and, implicitly, to serve as the final arbiter of the meaning of constitutional provisions. In time of emergency, the sovereign also had the power to declare martial law and to restrict his subjects' freedoms by decree.

The historical significance of the Principles, however, did not lie in the hedges and limits it contained. What was important was that the sovereign, although retaining ultimate power, voluntarily recognized certain rights and agreed to codify their practice in laws, which he offered not to alter without seeking the advice of parliament. He promised to give subjects access to the courts and said that court decisions based on law would not be lightly interfered with by administrative fiat. Predictability and regularity had been pursued by earlier dynasties in the form of respect for precedent. Now for the first time an emperor committed himself to give special solemnity to a class of enactments called laws, and to include subjects' rights among the matters treated in these protected enactments. Thus reassured and guided, the people were expected to contribute their energies to the imperial project of strengthening the nation. The authors of the Principles did not envision that citizens might want to use rights in an adversarial manner against the ruler or that the ruler might want to manipulate the legislative process or the judicial system to empty rights of their substance. They had drafted a compact for cooperation between state and people, not for conflict.

Before the constitution envisioned in the Principles could be implemented, the dynasty fell. An assembly of provincial delegates drew up a Provisional Constitution for the new republic. The Provisional Constitution, the never-enacted Temple of Heaven Draft (1913), and the Constitution of 1923 which replaced the Provisional Constitution, were the three major texts of the early republican period, similar enough to be discussed together.

Befitting the constitutions of a new republic the three texts gave political rights more positive emphasis than the Principles. The first two articles of the Provisional Constitution stated that "the Chinese Republic is made up of the Chinese people" and "the sovereignty of the Chinese Republic resides in the entire body of the citizenry." After two more introductory articles, the text turned directly to a chapter entitled "The People" (*renmin*). Among its eleven articles were the following political rights:

> *Article 5.* The people of the Chinese Republic are all equal, without differences of race, class, or religion.
> *Article 6.* The people enjoy the following freedoms:
> . . . 4. The people have the freedoms of speech, writing, publication, and of assembly and association.
> 5. The people have the freedom of confidentiality of correspondence. . . .
> *Article 7.* The people have the right to petition the parliament.
> *Article 8.* The people have the right to appeal to administrative offices.
> *Article 9.* The people have the right to appeal to the courts and receive court judgment.
> *Article 10.* The people have the right to appeal to the Supreme [Administrative] Court actions by officials which are illegal or deleterious to their rights.
> *Article 11.* The people have the right to take civil service examinations.
> *Article 12.* The people have the right to vote and to be candidates for office.

Compared to the Principles, the Provisional Constitution mentioned four rights of appeal and petition instead of one; it specified the equality of citizens and the concept of popular sovereignty, and it added the right of secrecy of correspondence. (Other nonpolitical rights were also added. Some rights were referred to as "rights" [*quan*] and some as "freedoms" [*ziyou*], a distinction without legal significance.) The Temple of Heaven Draft and the 1923 constitution contained virtually the same list of political rights. Rights were no longer the emperor's grant. The Provisional Constitution said rights were enjoyed by "the people," and the more carefully written Temple Draft changed this to "citizens" (*guomin*). The Temple Draft defined citizen (*minguo renmin*) as "anyone legally holding Chinese nationality."

The Provisional Constitution stated that "the people's rights . . . may be limited by law if doing so is deemed to advance the public welfare, to uphold order, or to be necessitated by an extraordinary emergency." The Temple Draft and the 1923 constitution dropped this provision, but included in each rights article the phrase "may not be restricted except by law," specifying no purposes that such legal restriction must serve. The Temple Draft also gave the president the power to issue orders having the force of law—and thus possibly restricting rights—in times of emergency or in order to maintain public order. In practice, early republican governments continued the Qing tradition of adopting laws and regulations that substantially restricted certain rights. For example, Yuan Shikai promulgated a publication law in 1914 that closely resembled the restrictive Qing law on the same subject.[13]

An unusual feature of the Temple Draft was that it recognized residual freedoms. Article 14 specified that "the freedoms of citizens of the Republic of China besides those specified in this chapter shall be recognized, provided they do not contradict the principles of constitutional government." Only the 1946 constitution contained a similar article. Had the provision come to a test, which it did not in the 1923 constitution's brief life, it presumably would have meant only that the government had to use the form of law to restrict freedoms not specified in the constitution, as it did those explicitly listed.

Popular sovereignty under the three texts was exercised through parliament, which among other powers could elect the president and vice president, approve the president's cabinet nominees and other high officials, interpellate and impeach, approve the budget, declare war and make treaties of peace, and pass laws. The Parliamentary Organic and Election Laws of 1912 established that the upper house was indirectly elected by the provincial assemblies, while the lower house was chosen from among their own number by members of provincial electoral colleges chosen in direct elections. Voters' qualifications were loosened from Qing days, producing an all-male electorate of about 10 percent of the population.[14] The parliament elected in 1912–1913 had a tumultuous history, meeting intermittently in various places until it was dissolved for good in 1924. A rival parliament was also elected under the Provisional Constitution in 1918 and lasted until 1920. Neither parliament proved able to exercise much power in the face of financial and military domination of government by warlords and politicians outside the legislature. Both eventually lost whatever popular mandates they had in displays of corruption and factional infighting.[15]

To protect his rights, the citizen could in principle appeal to courts or administrative offices against the acts of individual bureaucrats. But under the chaotic conditions of the warlord period few courts were established and their authority seldom reached far. Both the Temple Draft and the 1923 text provided that any law that contradicted the constitution would be invalid, with determinations of which laws fell into this category to be made by a constitutional convention composed of the members of parliament. This aspect of the early republican constitutions resembled the idea of parliamentary supremacy in England. But China lacked the traditions that eventually accumulated in England to check parliamentary abuse of personal rights, such as the doctrine of "rule of law" and the system of mass democracy. The early republican parliaments in fact passed few laws of any kind, simply because they were so disorganized. Nor did parliament ever exercise its power to declare a law unconstitutional.

The Guomindang Period

A theme already visible in the early constitutions is that the harmony of interests between state and citizen makes it unnecessary to conceive of rights as high-priority claims of individuals against the state. Instead, they are privileges granted by the state which the state can define and modify by law. This line of thought was further developed in the theory of single-party "tutelage" put forward by the Guomindang (Kuomintang, or Nationalist Party), which came to power in 1927–1928. According to the party's founder, Sun Yat-sen, China was so backward that democracy would have to be introduced gradually from the local level up, in step with economic development and the spread of education. This process must be overseen by a politically advanced ruling party.[16] In 1931 the Guomindang convened a national convention to adopt a Provisional Constitution for the Tutelage Period, or Tutelage Constitution. It was to be replaced by a permanent constitution once the people had reached the economic, educational, and political level necessary for constitutional government.

The Tutelage Constitution, like its predecessors, placed a bill of rights near the beginning of the text. The rights to take civil service examinations and to serve in public offices were listed. So were the freedoms to speak, publish, assemble, and associate. The freedom to write mentioned in earlier constitutions was implicit in the freedom to "publish writings." Three rights of petition or appeal were specified. Correspondence both by letter and by telegram were granted confidentiality. The constitution recognized the equality before the law of all citizens without regard to race, religion, and class just as did earlier constitutions, but added for the first time equality irrespective of gender.

The text used the terms "citizens" and "people" almost interchangeably. Not stated in the document was the ruling party's interpretation of the concept of "citizen." In January 1924, the party had stated in the declaration of its First National Congress:

This party's concept of "people's power" (*minquan zhuyi*) is different from the idea of so-called "natural rights." We advocate whatever is suitable to the present needs of the Chinese revolution. Now democratic rights in a republic should be enjoyed only by the citizens of the republic; they must not be carelessly bestowed on persons who oppose the republic and who would use them to wreck it. In China's case this means that all freedoms and rights may be enjoyed by any groups and individuals who authentically oppose imperialism; but groups and individuals who sell out the country and deceive the people on behalf of imperialism and the warlords are not to enjoy these freedoms and rights.[17]

Earlier constitutions had granted rights not to all persons within the country but to holders of Chinese citizenship; now Guomindang ideology proposed a loyalty test as an additional requirement for full citizenship. As one GMD-affiliated political scientist put it in 1928, "Only the Three People's Principles can now save China.

So only the supporters of the Three People's Principles should have rights."[18] To enforce this principle, the party's third congress in 1929 resolved that all citizens should be required to support the party and swear a loyalty oath to the Three People's Principles as conditions for being allowed to exercise their citizens' rights. The loyalty oath apparently was never put systematically into effect, although it found its way into several pieces of legislation.[19] Unlike the later communist regime, the nationalist government did not go beyond the oath in establishing procedures to deprive of political rights those who failed to share the official ideology.

The Tutelage Constitution followed the precedent of earlier constitutions by including in each rights article the phrase "according to law" to indicate how the right or freedom should be exercised or could be limited. The 1935 criminal code, the 1937 revised press law, and other laws put this principle into practice. They proscribed among other things the sale or display of "indecent" writings or pictures and the appearance in publications or the movies of ideas contrary to the Three People's Principles. Both films and the press were subject to prior censorship from the late 1920s on, with the censorship becoming increasingly heavy-handed after the Sino-Japanese war started in 1937.[20]

In addition to continuing the general legal authority to limit rights, the constitution limited certain rights in some specific ways of its own. While earlier constitutions listed such duties as paying taxes and doing military service, the Tutelage Constitution listed a new obligation for citizens "to obey public officials in the legal discharge of their public duties." Freedom of speech so far as it might concern teaching was partially modified by an article in the chapter on "Citizen Education" that stated, "public and private educational institutions throughout the country will be supervised by the state and have the obligation to carry out the educational policy set by the state."

The Tutelage Constitution accepted the principle of popular sovereignty, but restricted participation to the local level for the duration of the tutelage period:

> *Article 7.* In counties that are completely self-governing as
> specified in Article 8 of [Sun Yat-sen's] *Principles of*

> *National Reconstruction*, citizens of the Republic of China
> enjoy the rights of election, recall, initiative, and ref-
> erendum as specified in Article 9 of those *Principles*.

In fact not a single county reached the stage of self-government envisioned in Sun Yat-sen's program during the time the Tutelage Constitution was in effect.[21] Meanwhile, the leaders of the national government were appointed by the ruling party's Central Executive Committee, and both the executive and the legislature were dominated by the party.[22] The constitution provided for a national assembly to meet and draft a permanent constitution. It was to be elected under universal and direct suffrage, but the election procedure was under complete party control. The election was carried out under unstable political conditions in most regions in 1936, but the assembly was not convened until 1946, its membership enlarged with several hundred government and minority party appointees. In 1938 the regime also convened a People's Political Council, consisting partly of Guomindang appointees and partly of persons elected by Guomindang-dominated political councils in the provinces. As it varied its institutional arrangements from time to time, the government in fact paid little attention to the constitution and tended to follow more closely another law it had promulgated, the Organic Law of the National Government. In short, according to the constitutional scholar Ch'ien Tuan-sheng, "The Tutelage Constitution was . . . ordained only to be ignored."[23]

The Tutelage Constitution gave the power to interpret the constitution to the Central Executive Committee of the Guomindang. So the ruling party that had written the constitution both controlled the government and interpreted the constitution. Despite the facilities for legalized repression implied in this and other provisions, the government and various party factions engaged in many acts of extralegal political repression before and after the promulgation of the constitution, including assassinations, illegal arrests, torture, summary executions, surprise searches of campuses, and terrorization of the press and intellectuals.[24] Liberals like Hu Shi, who had pressed for a constitution in order to secure protection for civil rights, found the constitution less useful in protecting rights than they had hoped.[25]

The period of tutelage formally came to an end with the adoption of a permanent constitution on December 25, 1946, and its promulgation the following January 1.[26] The 1946 constitution is still in effect in Taiwan. Party dictatorship was absent from the 1946 constitution. The first article described the state as a "democratic republic of the people, for the people, and governed by the people," and the second vested sovereignty in "the whole body of the citizens." No party was given a special role. Citizens were guaranteed equality before the law without regard to religion, race, class, and gender, and without regard to party affiliation as well. On the other hand, the orthodoxy of Sun Yatsenism was enshrined both in the preamble and in article 1, which stated that "the Republic of China is founded on the Three People's Principles."

Rights and freedoms received here the most generous treatment given in any Chinese constitution. This was the only one whose preamble listed "protection of the people's rights" as a goal of government alongside collective goods like strengthening the state and promoting social welfare. Following tradition, the 1946 constitution placed its chapter on the rights and duties of the people near the head of the text. All the political rights and freedoms listed in earlier constitutions were repeated. These included the freedoms to speak, write, publish, assemble and associate, and the secrecy of correspondence. A new freedom, that of teaching and learning (*jiangxue*), was added, but was qualified by a provision that "education and culture should promote citizens' national spirit and their spirit of self-government, their civic morality, their physical health, and scientific and practical knowledge." In the 1946 constitution article 22 restored the concept of residual freedoms introduced in the 1923 constitution: "All other freedoms and rights of the people that are not deleterious to the social order and the public interest shall receive the protection of the constitution."

Suspicion of bureaucracy had been evident in all previous constitutions. The Qing Principles granted citizens a right to be heard in court, apparently so they could appeal cases of bureaucratic oppression. The Provisional Constitution specified four different rights of petition or suit; the 1923 constitution two types; the Tutelage Constitution three types. The 1946 constitution not only granted "all persons the rights to petition, to file administrative appeals, and to institute legal proceedings," but it added:

> *Article 24.* Any public official who illegally infringes on the people's freedoms or rights shall not only receive disciplinary punishments according to law but shall also be held responsible under criminal and civil laws. The injured person may, in accordance with law, apply to the state for compensation for the damages sustained.

It was not until 1980, however, that the government (by then in Taiwan) enacted the State Compensation Law needed to give force to this article.[27]

The provision in a number of earlier constitutions that each freedom or right must be exercised or could be restricted "according to law" had been much criticized on the ground that "the constitutional law gave freedom with the one hand and took it back with the other."[28] The 1946 constitution no longer inserted this phrase in each article. Instead it contained a separate article 23, which specified that "the freedoms and rights listed in the various articles above may not be restricted by law except as necessary to prevent damage to the freedoms of others, avert an imminent crisis, maintain social order, or promote the common good." The negative form of the statement, the priority it gave to protecting the "freedoms of others," and its segregation in one article implied that government should be more cautious about restricting rights than it had been in the past. But the article still gave sufficient room to justify any restriction of rights based on properly adopted law. The criminal law, press law, and other existing laws and rules restricting rights continued in effect after 1946. In May 1949 the nationalist Garrison Command in Taiwan declared a state of siege which brought into effect martial law regulations suspending all constitutional civil rights. The constitutional basis claimed for the state of siege was the president's power to declare martial law under the 1946 constitution, but, as Ming-min Peng and others have pointed out, the procedures used to impose it were not those the constitution required.[29] The state of siege still exists in Taiwan, buttressed by a number of new enactments restricting political rights. However, the nationalist government has claimed that the actual impact of martial law on most citizens' political freedom has been modest.[30]

The 1946 constitution's provisions for the exercise of popular sovereignty were more complete in design than those in any other Chinese constitution before or since. A directly elected National Assembly had the power to elect and recall the president and vice president and to amend the constitution. A directly elected Legislative Yuan was to pass on laws, the budget, war and peace, and so on. The Control Yuan, in charge of supervision and audit of the bureaucracy, was indirectly elected through provincial and municipal councils that were directly elected. All elections were to be based on universal suffrage, open campaigns, and the secret ballot; all elected candidates could be recalled; a quota of women to be elected was to be fixed by law for each elected institution. The National Assembly was elected in 1947 and the Legislative Yuan in 1948 in nationwide elections that were somewhat competitive despite Guomindang efforts at control. The Control Yuan was elected in 1948. The National Assembly discharged its constitutional duty by confirming Chiang Kai-shek as president in the same year. Despite these elaborate representative institutions, the personal dominance of Chiang Kai-shek and later his son and the party dominance of the Guomindang remained unchecked. With the retreat of the nationalist government to Taiwan it became impossible to conduct further nationwide elections, so the old National Assembly, Legislative Yuan, and Control Yuan members have remained in office, supplemented by new members elected within the province in 1969 and later.[31]

The 1946 constitution contained the first and only provision for independent judicial review found in any Chinese constitution. No fewer than four articles made the point that laws and ordinances contrary to the constitution were null and void. This determination as well as interpretations of the constitution were to be made by a constitutional council consisting of the Grand Justices of the Judicial Yuan, who were required to be independent and above party and who held office for life. In practice, this power of judicial review has been exercised with extreme restraint. In the period 1949–1975 the Council of Grand Justices received 167 applications for constitutional decisions and ruled on 35 of them. In only one case did it declare a statute unconstitutional, a case involving the proper administrative line of supervision for lower courts. By 1980 the government still had not complied with the council's twenty-year-old decision in this matter. In this period the council did not rule in favor of any individual appeal against government actions.[32]

Innovations in the Jiangxi Program

From the 1930s on, a separate but in some ways similar constitutional tradition began to develop under the aegis of the Chinese Communist Party. Founded in 1921, the Party by 1931 ruled a base area in and around the province of Jiangxi where it founded a formal government, the Chinese Soviet Republic or Jiangxi Soviet. The Soviet's Constitutional Program, adopted in 1931 and revised in 1934, was modeled on the 1924 constitution of the USSR and, except for the 1930 draft described in Professor Edwards' essay, was the first crystallization of Chinese Communist political theory in the form of a basic law.[33] Like the Qing Principles, the Jiangxi Program was a brief outline for a full constitution to be developed later. Nonetheless its seventeen articles contained some important innovations for China.

First, sovereignty and political rights belonged neither to all the people nor to all the citizens of the Soviet Republic. Since Marxist theory regards the state as an instrument by which one class oppresses another, the laboring classes were to enjoy sovereignty and rights while the remnant elements of the old feudal and bourgeois orders were not. Article 2 provided:

Under Soviet rule all workers, peasants, red fighters [revolutionary army members], and members of the laboring masses have the power to elect delegates to manage the government. Only warlords, bureaucrats, landlords, evil gentry, capitalists, rich peasants, monks and priests, and all exploiters and counterrevolutionaries shall lack the right to vote for representatives to participate in political power and shall lack political freedoms.

Thus class rather than nationality or humanity was the qualification for enjoying political rights—so much so, in fact, that article 16 specifically stated, "the Chinese Soviet regime grants to foreigners residing in the Soviet areas who are engaged in labor the equal enjoyment of all political rights fixed in law." This extraordinary provision was not repeated in later Communist constitutions.

The principle of differential class access to political rights was a refinement of the Guomindang's theory that such rights should be withheld from citizens who did not share the ruling party's goals for the nation. Both parties' ideologies on this point were of Marxist-Leninist origin. But where the Guomindang advocated a loyalty oath, the Communists applied the more stringent test of class membership. This opened the way to a later reversal in the senses of the terms "people" and "citizens." In the past, "people" or "persons" (renmin) had been the more inclusive term, and most Chinese constitutions granted rights only to citizens. The Jiangxi program used neither term, granting rights instead to "workers" and "laboring masses," even of foreign nationality. By 1949 when a document called the Common Program was promulgated as a temporary constitution for the People's Republic, "citizens" had become the more inclusive term and "people" the more restrictive one. When the Common Program spoke of granting rights to "the people," it meant only that portion of the citizenry who were qualified by class standing to enjoy full membership in the state.

The Common Program read that "the people of the People's Republic of China shall enjoy freedom of thought, speech, publication," and so forth, while "all reactionary elements, feudal landlords, and bureaucratic capitalists . . . shall be deprived of their political rights in accordance with law for the period of time necessary."[34] As a PRC constitutional textbook explained, " 'The people' means the working class, the peasant class, the petty bourgeoisie, the national bourgeoisie and those patriotic elements who have consciously crossed over from the counterrevolutionary classes." The reactionary elements deprived of their rights "do not belong within the scope of the people although they are still Chinese citizens."[35] In subsequent PRC constitutions the term "people" continued to have this technical meaning. However, the specific groups included and excluded have varied over time because, as the PRC press has recently reiterated: " 'People' is primarily a historical concept and changes according to the economic conditions of society in different historical periods. At the same time, it is also a political concept and changes with every change in the character and tasks of the revolution."[36]

A second innovation of the Jiangxi Program was to present rights explicitly as goals to be realized in the future rather than as immediately effective claims. The preamble stated:

The Second National Congress of the Chinese Soviet hereby publishes to the laboring masses of China and the world the basic tasks which it seeks to accomplish in China. . . . These tasks have already begun to be carried out within the present Soviet areas. But the Second National Congress holds that the completion of these tasks must await the overthrow of imperialist and Guomindang rule in China and the establishment of the rule of the Soviet Republic throughout the country.

Article 10 elaborated:

The Chinese Soviet political power takes as a goal the guaranteeing of workers', peasants', and laboring masses' freedoms of speech, publication, assembly, and association. . . . It uses the force of the masses' political power to obtain printing facilities (newspapers, printing plants, etc.), meeting places, and all necessary facilities in order to give the workers, peasants, and laboring masses the material basis to guarantee their exercise of these rights.

This article listed political rights familiar from earlier Chinese constitutions—speech, publication, assembly, and association. It went beyond earlier texts in recognizing that material facilities were needed to make these rights into realities. But then it seemed to put off the enjoyment of the rights until the time when the material basis could be obtained. In terminology used later, rights were seen as "programmatic" (ganglingxing).

In a practical sense rights in earlier constitutions had been largely programmatic as well, since social and political conditions did not exist for them to be exercised by all who enjoyed them in principle. In addition, the Qing Principles and the 1931 Tutelage Constitution were programmatic documents by nature, the former because it laid down principles to be embodied in a later constitution, the latter because it was written to govern a transitional period during which the conditions for constitutional government were going to be built. And both the 1931 and the 1946 constitutions contained special chapters on the government's economic, social, and other policy goals. But in these texts—and in the other pre-Communist constitutions as well—the specific provisions describing rights were couched in the Chinese equivalent of present tense. The Jiangxi Program was the first constitutional document to extend the programmatic concept explicitly to rights. Its language thus made clearer than previous texts a philosophical conception of rights not as prior conditions of the citizen-state relationship but as benefits the government aimed to deliver, on a level with other policy goals such as peace, prosperity, and national pride. Later Communist-sponsored constitutions were also founded on the principle of expressing rights as goals rather than as claims. Speaking, for example, of the 1978 constitution, the Party journal *Red Flag* explained:

The fact that our constitution still cannot provide citizens with freedom of movement is due to the limits imposed by our level of economic development. Indeed, citizens' actual enjoyment and specific use of their [other] freedoms . . . are also all restricted to a certain extent by the societywide development levels of science and culture, political ideology, and morality. Therefore, only by conscientiously upholding the authority of socialist law and by working hard to promote economic and cultural development can we better protect and expand citizens' individual freedoms.[37]

Third, the Jiangxi Program contained a number of new political rights. Article 5 said that "workers have the right to supervise production"—a basis for communist-led trade unions to claim more influence in capitalist-owned enterprises of the day. Article 7 stated that the "right to shoulder arms to participate in the revolutionary struggle is limited to workers, peasants, and the laboring masses." Article 14 gave minority nationalities the right of "national self-determination even to the point of secession from China and establishment of their own independent states"—a provision repeated in no other Chinese constitution. Article 15 granted the right of asylum to Chinese or foreign "revolutionary fighters." As already noted, article 16 gave foreign laborers residing in the Soviet areas equal enjoyment of all political rights. There were also a number of new rights concerning women's affairs, education, and antireligious propaganda. The document failed to mention secrecy of correspondence and rights of appeal and petition, but this may have been due simply to its brevity, since those rights were included in some later Communist-drafted constitutions.

The profusion of rights outlined in the Jiangxi Program was linked with its programmatic nature. Since a constitution was a statement of goals and of policies to achieve them, as the political program changed, so did the rights that might be necessary to realize it. The forging of new political rights continued in subsequent Communist-sponsored constitutions. The 1946 Shaan-Gan-Ning Border Region Constitutional Principles contained the provision "The people have the right of armed self-defense, in such forms as self-defense armies and militia."[38] The 1949 Common Program stated, "the freedom to report the news truthfully shall be safeguarded." The 1975 PRC constitution introduced new rights of political expression and action called the "four great freedoms." In programmatic constitutions, in short, the list of rights might grow as the political tasks of the era dictated. By the same token, as we shall see, rights were dropped from one constitution to the next as the political need for them receded.

The Jiangxi Program's final innovation was an institutional form for the exercise of popular sovereignty: a Russian-style ascending series of soviets, each elected by the one below and each empowered to direct the administrative organs at its level. These "worker-peasant-soldier soviet congresses" were to be elected by secret and universal suffrage of the "laboring masses." The deputies were to maintain close contact with the units that elected them and were subject to recall. At the top was a National Congress of Soviets which was to exercise supreme state power on behalf of the masses. By 1932 soviets had been elected at village, district, and county levels in about sixty counties in the Jiangxi Soviet and affiliated Communist-controlled areas. The national congress met twice, in 1931 and 1934.[39] A similar governmental structure was later installed in the Shaan-Gan-Ning Border Region and other Communist base areas.[40]

In theory the system of soviets or councils was supposed to provide strong lines of control for the people over government. The Soviet and Chinese designers of the system had in mind Marx's praise for the Paris Commune of 1871 as a model of working-class democracy. Marx emphasized that the delegates to the commune were ordinary workingmen who served at working men's wages. They were elected by universal suffrage and subject to recall. The commune was not just a house of talk: it "was to be a working, not a parliamentary, body, executive and legislative at the same time."[41] In reality the Chinese soviets, like the Russian, were weak and met infrequently. The business of government was handled by bureaucrats who were responsive to and often members of the Communist Party.[42] The fact of Party control was mentioned nowhere in the Jiangxi Program or the Shaan-Gan-Ning Border Region Constitutional Principles, in part because these documents described the structure of governmental organs rather than those of the Party. But if one turned to the Party's own constitution, one found the party charging itself with the responsibility to "establish itself as the core of all revolutionary mass organizations and of the revolutionary organizations of the nation."[43]

Thus China's first Communist-sponsored constitutional document bore with it a classic Marxist contradiction between the aspiration for popular control and the need for Party leadership. A good Marxist would value both, but both could not be equally vigorous at the same time. To say that the Party represented the interests of the people could justify Party leadership but could not also fulfill the desire for actual popular control. In the Hundred Flowers Campaign of 1957 Chinese intellectuals, including many professing loyalty to Marxism, called for the Party to relinquish a large part of its political control to the people. Later Mao Zedong termed the masses "more progressive" than the party and summoned them to rise up and "topple" the party leaders. In 1978—

1981 the Democracy Movement and its sympathizers within the Party challenged the leaders to cede control over government to the people by instituting a free press and competitive elections. All these challenges were turned back by the Party, but they had their origins in the conception of proletarian democracy the Party itself had encouraged.[44]

The First Three PRC Constitutions

In 1954 the first full-fledged constitution under Communism was promulgated, replacing the 1949 Common Program.[45] In certain respects it set the pattern for the constitutions that followed—those of 1975, 1978, and 1982—despite important differences in their content, some of which are explored below. Each constitution started with a preamble characterizing the era and its tasks, and lauding the leadership of the party. Each had a first chapter on general policies, particularly in the realm of the economy. All four described the social class composition of "the people," in whom sovereignty was vested, in the same way ("led by the working class and based on the alliance of workers and peasants"). Each granted rights to "citizens," a broader category than "the people," but provided for some citizens who were not members of the people to be deprived of political rights (although in 1982 for the first time such deprivation was not imposed on whole classes).

The guiding purpose of the 1954 constitution was to rally support and unify energies for the task of economic construction. As Mao explained: "This is a constitution for the transition period. We must now unite the people of the whole country and unite all the forces that can and should be united in the struggle to build a great socialist country. And the constitution has been drawn up specifically for this purpose."[46] Chapter 1 accordingly listed the state's current economic policies, and chapter 2, the bulk of the document, described the state's institutional structure. The chapter on citizens' rights and duties was placed near the end of the text. As Li Da, an official commentator, explained, "The nature of the citizens' basic rights and duties as set down in our state constitution is determined by our country's social system and state institutional system."[47] Where the republican constitutions had purported to fit the institutions of the state to citizens' rights, rights were now framed to suit the purposes of the state, and the order of priority was accordingly reversed in the text.

In the tradition of the Jiangxi Program, many rights in the 1954 constitution and in subsequent PRC constitutions were programmatic. The 1954 constitution spoke, for example, of "providing the necessary material facilities" for certain rights (art. 87), of protecting rights by laws yet to be passed (art. 90), and of "gradually expanding" the material facilities to guarantee certain rights (arts. 91, 92, 93, 94). Mao explained: "We write into our constitution what is feasible now and exclude what is not. Let us take for instance the material guarantees for civil rights. They will certainly expand when production grows in future, but the wording in the constitution is only 'gradually expand.' This, too, means flexibility."[48] Li Da elaborated: "The rules on citizens' basic rights and duties in the constitution use the form of law to summarize the rights and freedoms that the people already have as well as their new extensions, and also to guarantee that they will continue to develop. . . . [These provisions] on the one hand sum up already existing realities in our country's life and on the other hand point the direction for future efforts."[49]

The four PRC constitutions varied in the rights they listed. The 1954 constitution was more cautious than the Jiangxi Program in granting political rights. It specified the rights of speech, publication, and assembly and association; the freedom to write was implicit in the newly stated "freedom . . . to engage in scientific research, literary and artistic creation, and other cultural activities." Freedoms of procession and demonstration were added. There was a right to appeal against state officials and a right to compensation for loss suffered at the hands of state employees acting in disregard of a citizen's rights. Secrecy of correspondence, absent from the Jiangxi Program, was restored. Equality before the law, the right to vote and to run for office, and popular sovereignty (meaning sovereignty of the progressive classes) were cited as in most previous constitutions. The people were granted a new but vague right to supervise state organs: "All organs of state must rely on the masses of the people, constantly maintain close contact with them, heed their opinions, and accept their supervision." Supervision by the workers in capitalist enterprises was mentioned as in the Jiangxi Program, not as a right but in the context of the state policy of "using" and "transforming" these enterprises. Political asylum was also carried over from the Jiangxi Program. But the new text deleted some of the Program's other innovations such as the right to participate in armed revolution and the right of national minorities to self-determination. The minorities retained the much weaker and ill-defined right of "autonomy," meaning limited self-rule within the larger state system. Nor did the 1954 constitution adopt the Guomindang constitutions' rights to initiative and referendum or the concept of residual rights found in the 1923 and 1946 texts.

Some earlier constitutions had stated that rights could be restricted by law in order to serve the common good, or had allowed rights to be exercised only in accordance with law. The 1954 constitution did not grant this power of restriction to the lawmakers in so many words, but the government did exercise it under both the 1954 and subsequent texts. By 1954 a number of rights had already been the subject of legislative or administrative regulation, and additional laws and regulations would follow. For example, the 1951 state secrets regulations limited free speech and the freedom of the press by defining state secrets as including "all state affairs which have not yet been decided upon or . . . have not yet been made public" and "all other state affairs which should be kept secret."[50] The 1952 regulations on book and periodical publishing required registration of all publishing enterprises and forbade publication of materials "that violate the Common Program . . . or the decrees of the Government," that are "prohibited by express Government decree," or "that disclose state secrets."[51] The rights of association, assembly, and speech could not be used to oppose the regime under the 1951 law against counterrevolutionaries.[52] The sale of books and pictures deemed "reactionary, obscene, or absurd" could be punished by police fines or short detentions under the Security Administration Punishment Act of 1957.[53] "Counterrevolutionaries and antisocialist reactionaries" whose "crimes are minor" could be sentenced by police administrative decision to three-year labor camp terms under the 1957 State Council Decision on Rehabilitation Through Labor.[54]

Besides the unwritten power to define and restrict rights, the state had the power under the 1954 constitution to deprive both individuals and classes of individuals of political rights. Rights were granted in the first instance to Chinese "citizens." But article 19 stated that "the state deprives feudal landlords and bureaucratic capitalists of political rights for a specific period of time according to law." The logic of this article followed that of the Jiangxi Program. Feudal landlords and bureaucratic capitalists were citizens but not members of the people. No longer among the ruling classes, they were classes ruled over, and as such could not participate in the exercise of political rights until they had been individually "reformed" and made into laboring people. They could, however, enjoy such nonpolitical rights as freedom of religious belief.

Deprivation of political rights had been used as a light supplemental penalty against "counterrevolutionaries" and other political opponents in the Jiangxi Soviet period and in the Shaan-Gan-Ning Border Region in the late 1940s.[55] The 1954 constitution extended the penalty from individuals to classes. In the process of land reform from 1946 to 1952, each person residing in the countryside had been given a class status (*jieji chengfen*) based upon his chief source of livelihood in the preceding three years. A similar although less thorough process had occurred in the cities. The process was inexact; as late as 1980, appeals were being heard to overturn erroneous classifications made in the 1950s.[56] Once classified as being of "bad class background" the individual had been automatically deprived of his or her political rights. Article 19 retroactively confirmed this classwide deprivation. The next two PRC constitutions contained similar articles, the 1975 version adding "rich peasants" and "other bad elements" to the deprived classes.

At the same time, Communist legal theorists continued

to hold that an individual, even of good class background, could lose his standing as a member of the people through criminal or political actions. The journal *Legal Research* explained in 1980, "When individuals within the people, influenced by the exploiting class ideology, commit outrages and antagonize the people, they may transform from the objects of democracy to those of dictatorship."[57] "Objects of democracy" means members of the people, while "those of dictatorship" means enemies of the people. Hence the new regime continued the practice of using deprivation of political rights as a supplemental criminal sanction. The sanction was employed in three sets of administrative regulations issued in the early 1950s against counterrevolutionaries, currency manipulators, and persons guilty of corruption. It was also retained for certain crimes in the criminal code of 1979.

To complicate matters further, deprivation of political rights has also been used as a penalty against victims of political movements, such as the Antirightist Movement of 1957 and the Great Proletarian Cultural Revolution of 1966–69. The "bad class elements" uncovered in these and other campaigns were often sent to prisons or labor camps or were kept at home under "control" or doing "supervised labor." Deprivation of political rights was imposed either formally or informally as a concomitant of general pariah status. The political ban was also commonly extended to the banned person's spouse and children. There are no accurate figures on the total number of persons affected. The Chinese press revealed in 1984 that four categories of persons "labeled" in the early 1950s—landlords, rich peasants, counterrevolutionaries, and bad elements—alone numbered more than twenty million. Additional millions, or tens of millions, were labeled in the Antirightist Movement, the Socialist Education Campaign, and the Cultural Revolution. Hu Yaobang, then general secretary of the Chinese Communist Party, told a group of Yugoslav journalists in 1980 that some 100 million people, one-tenth of the Chinese population, had to be rehabilitated to undo the effects of the Cultural Revolution and previous campaigns.[58] We do not know how many of these cases involved deprivation of political rights.

The rights of which people were deprived varied over

time and from case to case. The 1951 regulations on the punishment of counterrevolutionaries defined political rights to include the rights to vote and be elected, to serve in government posts, to participate in people's organizations and the militia, to receive national honors and decorations, and the freedoms of speech, publication, assembly, association, correspondence, residence and change of residence, and demonstration. In other enactments the list was shorter, and depending on the severity of their crimes individuals might be deprived of only some, not all, of the rights on the list. Practical reality was still more complicated than legal theory. During much of PRC history there were in effect no political rights to be deprived of—no elections, private publications, associations or demonstrations, and no chance to change residence. Under these conditions loss of political rights was more important as a symbol of social ostracism and downward social mobility than as a deprivation in itself. The treatment of "bad elements" varied from place to place and time to time. They might be severely punished or, especially in big cities, ignored and overlooked. Although the constitution authorized deprivation "for a specific period of time according to law," which legal scholars understood to mean a ban of one to five years' duration,[59] a political ban generally continued until someone took the initiative to lift it. Some bans were lifted as categories of individuals were rehabilitated, but apparently in the great majority of cases indecision by the central government or local officials meant that the penalty continued until the large-scale rehabilitation that began in 1977 and continued into the 1980s.

In the matter of institutions for the exercise of popular sovereignty, the 1954 constitution also followed the lead of the Jiangxi Program. It established a hierarchy of people's congresses from the village or urban district level up to the national level, with the lowest congresses elected by universal adult suffrage except for persons deprived of political rights.[60] The National People's Congress elected and could remove from office all the major officials of the executive and judicial branches and had the power to decide on legislation, the national economic plan, the budget, war and peace, and other matters. But the congresses were de-

signed as something less than Marx's "working body, both executive and legislative." The NPC was required to meet only once
a year (though its standing committee might meet more often), and
substantial administrative responsibilities were assigned to the state
chairman, the prime minister, and the cabinet (state council). Local-level governments were supposed to be responsible not only
to the people's congresses that elected them but to higher administrative levels as well. With these qualifications, the constitution
followed in form the modified Paris Commune model—a single,
clear line of authority from the people, with no separation of powers. As in the Jiangxi period, the responsibility for the CCP to lead
the state was written into the CCP constitution, not that of the
state.[61]

In fact, CCP domination of the people's congresses and
other organs of state was complete. Basic-level congress elections
were held six times between 1953 and 1966. The voters in each
constituency faced a single slate of candidates put forward by a
nominating committee controlled by party members. Most people's
congress members were cadres and party members reelected again
and again, as were the state chairman, prime minister, and other
high officials at the national level. The power of recall was seldom
if ever used at any level. Local congress meetings were brief and
uneventful. National congresses were generally preceded by meetings of the CCP Central Committee and invariably gave unanimous
approval to the draft legislation and personnel nominations the
Central Committee submitted to them. The NPC met for about two
weeks at a time, once a year, from 1954 to 1964–65 with the
exception of 1961. The congress was not convened again until
January 1975. Reviewing this history in 1980, the deputy head of
the Central Party School, Feng Wenbin, admitted that so far "democracy is a mere formality in our country; in practice, only a few
people have a say in the government." A legal journal added that
"people's congresses have not played their role as organs of state
power as they should."[62]

Like earlier Chinese constitutions, the 1954 constitution contained no effective provision for enforcing its supremacy
over laws or administrative actions that might violate it. The courts

and procuracy were appointed by and accountable to the people's congresses. The judiciary was declared "independent, subject only to law"—language which left no room for counterposing constitutional guarantees against restrictions enacted in law. The procuracy could protest violations of law but could neither annul such government acts nor argue that a law contravened the constitution.[63] As in earlier constitutions, the power to assure that laws conformed to the constitution lay with the legislative organs themselves. The relevant provisions were never actually used to protect citizens in the exercise of their rights. Instead, from 1957 on the powers of the courts and procuracy declined, and after 1961 neither the NPC, its standing committee, nor the local congresses were able to meet. During the Cultural Revolution all semblance of orderly constitutional procedure, including protection of political rights, was abandoned.

By 1969 it was possible to convene a Party congress (the first since 1956), but the state apparatus continued to function in effect without a fundamental law. The 1954 constitution was neither withdrawn nor obeyed; no one referred to it. In 1970 a constitutional draft was circulated but not adopted, apparently because of political disagreements among the leaders.[64] It took until 1975 for a new constitution to be adopted, and then it was replaced in quick succession by those of 1978 and 1982.[65]

Promulgated in the next-to-last year of Mao Zedong's life, the 1975 constitution was intended to be part of his legacy to his ideological heirs. If the chief task in 1954 had been to unite the people for the transition to socialism, in 1975 the preamble hailed an era when socialist society had already been built. But citing a pessimistic theory that Mao had developed in the 1960s, it added that in socialist society "there are classes, class contradictions and class struggle, there is the struggle between the socialist road and the capitalist road, there is the danger of capitalist restoration." Hence the main task in the socialist era was described as vigilant defense of the revolution through class struggle. What this meant in practice was that the police and the Party should weed out all who were skeptical of Mao's policies, punish them, and try to reeducate them. For this purpose the Party must closely control the state apparatus. The new constitution mentioned Party leadership four times in its preamble and several times in the main text. Its length was reduced from 106 articles to 30, on the grounds that practical details could be left to be decided by the Party.

The 1975 constitution repeated many of the now-standard political rights—the rights to free speech, publication, assembly, association, appeal against the conduct of state employees, procession and demonstration, national minority autonomy, and political asylum for foreign revolutionaries. It also made some interesting additions. It added the right to strike, proposed by Mao in 1956 when he said it would "help resolve the contradictions between the state and the factory director on the one hand and the masses of workers on the other."[66] And it enshrined the so-called "four great freedoms" which Mao had codified and which had been widely exercised during the Cultural Revolution: "Speaking out freely, airing views fully, holding great debates, and writing big-character posters are new forms of socialist revolution created by the masses of the people. The state shall ensure to the masses the right to use these forms."

The growing dominance of the Party was reflected in restrictions and deletions in political rights provisions. The article just quoted granted the masses the right to exercise the "four great freedoms," but went on to specify that these forms should be used only in such a way as to "help consolidate the leadership of the Communist Party of China over the state." The 1954 article safeguarding the freedom of scientific research, literary and artistic creation, and other cultural activities was recast into a requirement that all cultural activity "serve proletarian politics, serve the workers, peasants and soldiers, and be combined with productive labor." Citizens' duties were now listed in the first article of the chapter on rights and duties, and where the 1954 constitution had mentioned a duty of all citizens to obey the constitution and the law, the 1975 constitution added a duty "to support the leadership of the Communist Party of China [and] support the socialist system." The masses' right to supervise state organs, which had been an innovation in the 1954 constitution, was attenuated in the 1975 text: "State organizations and state personnel must . . . maintain close ties with the masses and wholeheartedly serve the people." The 1975 text deleted the 1954 reference to workers' supervision in factories, since there were no longer any capitalist-owned factories. It deleted the right to compensation for loss suffered by citizens as a consequence of state employees' infringements of their rights. It deleted the right to privacy of correspondence, thus bringing constitutional language into line with the police practice of opening people's mail.[67] Freedom of correspondence was still listed, however.

Finally, this was the first constitution since the fall of the Qing to contain no reference to equality before the law. By 1975 the number had grown very large of persons suffering political and economic discrimination as a result of their own or their parents' "bad class status" or of having been labeled in campaigns. The authors of the 1975 constitution regarded the existence of this political underclass as a necessary consequence of revolutionary vigilance. As Zhang Chunqiao put it in his report to the NPC on the new text, "The class nature of our state and the status of each class in our country are clearly defined. . . . Our draft adheres to this principled stand of Marxism-Leninism and is sharply demarcated from such fallacies as Confucius' 'benevolent government' or the Soviet revisionist renegade clique's 'state of the whole people.' "[68] Equality before the law was not regarded as an appropriate principle for a revolutionary society.

The 1975 constitution contained the same language as the 1954 constitution about the citizen's right to vote and retained the system of people's congresses, although specifying for the first time in a state constitution the principle of Communist Party leadership over the NPC. The method of selection of people's congress deputies, however, was now described as "democratic consultation" rather than "election." This gave sanction to a practice long followed in people's congress elections, whereby the party-dominated election committee presented a candidate list equal in number to the number of seats to be filled. The list was supposed to be a product of wide-ranging discussions about the merits of potential candidates and was supposed to represent a popular consensus. The authors of the 1975 text seemed to feel that it was no longer necessary to confirm the consensus list through the formality of voting. But later Chinese reports charged that little negotiation went on before the presentation of these lists to the public; often "democratic consultation" consisted of nothing more than a ten-minute presentation of names followed by a show of hands.[69]

On the subject of constitutional review the 1975 constitution followed the 1954 precedent fairly closely. The National People's Congress had the power to amend the constitution, although no longer to supervise its enforcement; the NPC standing committee had the power to interpret laws, although no longer the power to annul administrative decisions that contravened the constitution. Local people's congresses were still charged with safeguarding the rights of citizens. The 1954 reference to the independence of the judiciary was dropped.

The 1978 constitution, adopted about a year and a half after Mao's death, reflected a state of political play in which the newly resurgent Deng Xiaoping had only partly rid the leadership of Mao's loyalists. The preamble echoed that of 1975 on the need for revolutionary vigilance but added a reference to the task of the four modernizations and called for "expanding" the united front, a hint of coming efforts to rehabilitate the millions labeled during political campaigns. But meanwhile the provision depriving landlords, rich peasants, and capitalists of political rights was retained, and the constitution added a promise to punish all "newborn bourgeois elements," broadly identified elsewhere as "embezzlers, thieves, speculators, swindlers, murderers, arsonists, gangsters, smash-and-grabbers, and other evildoers."[70] The dominance of the Chinese Communist Party over the state was mentioned, but in fewer places, and not in the section on the NPC. The constitution was doubled in size to sixty articles, suggesting a renewed sense that the state apparatus needed its own procedures even if ultimately answerable to the Party.

The 1978 constitution continued to set a disciplined tone for the exercise of rights. The requirement for citizens to support CCP leadership was set into a separate article and exanded:

> *Article 56.* Citizens must support the leadership of the Communist Party of China, support the socialist system, safe-

guard the unification of the motherland [that is, accept government policies on the Taiwan issue] and the unity of all nationalities in our country and abide by the Constitution and the law.

The next article added, among others, duties to "respect social ethics and safeguard state secrets." There was a hint of a policy of cultural thaw—although certainly no promise of a right to cultural freedom—in the passage "The state applies the policy of 'letting a hundred flowers blossom and a hundred schools of thought contend' so as to promote the development of the arts and sciences and bring about a flourishing socialist culture" (art. 14). But the 1975 requirement for cultural activities to serve the proletariat was expanded to three articles in 1978, touching respectively on science, education, and culture, which were all required to serve socialism and to accept "the leading position of Marxism-Leninism—Mao Zedong Thought." The "four great freedoms" introduced in 1975 were retained. But in 1980 in a rare exercise of the amendment power, the National People's Congress deleted them on the suggestion of the Party Central Committee, on the grounds that they were unnecessarily contentious forms of democracy that had been used during and after the Cultural Revolution to attack people rather than for legitimate political expression.[71] The deletion was a riposte to the Democracy Movement which in 1978 and 1979 had used wall posters to express a variety of grievances and demands for reform.

The 1978 constitution contained evidence of the leadership's renewed concern with the immobility and unresponsiveness of the bureaucracy. Not only was the people's right to supervise the bureaucracy restored, but it was repeated in three articles and expanded beyond its 1954 level. Article 15 required organs of state "to rely on" and "heed" the masses, article 16 called on them to "serve" and "accept supervision by" the masses, and article 17 read "the state adheres to the principle of socialist democracy, and ensures to the people the right to participate in the management of state affairs and of all economic and cultural undertakings, and the right to supervise the organs of state and their personnel." Among other implications, this article seemed at least in part to restore the workers' right to supervise production found in the 1954 constitution. Even if "all economic . . . undertakings" were interpreted as covering only state industrial enterprises, it would include some 84,000 state-owned factories employing almost 80 percent of the industrial work force.[72] Indeed, in 1981, regulations were promulgated providing for election of workers' and staff congresses in state-owned industrial enterprises.[73]

A final check on the bureaucracy was provided in article 55, which established the citizen's right of appeal in two different ways. The 1975 constitution had said that citizens could lodge written or oral complaints about state employees' behavior to organs of state at any level. The 1978 constitution repeated this and added that citizens could also appeal to organs of state at any level against any infringement of their rights. The added language implied protection from infringements by other persons as well as by state employees. Both article 55 and article 17 were given substance when the party in 1979 launched a campaign to revitalize the tradition of "letters and visits work" (xinfang gongzuo), whereby most government and Party offices, including the police, set up special sections to handle individuals' petitions and complaints submitted in person or by letter.[74]

The 1978 constitution preserved the people's congress system and restored the principle of election of deputies "after democratic consultation." In 1979 the NPC adopted new people's congress organic and electoral laws to replace those of 1953–54. These extended the principle of direct election beyond the basic-level congresses (communes and towns) to include the next-higher county and city-district level congresses, as a step toward direct election of congresses at all levels. Moreover, in these elections the number of candidates on the election committee's final list was required to be one-and-a-half to two times the number of seats to be filled, and the competing candidates were allowed a five-day campaign period to explain their qualifications and views to the voters. Election was to be by secret ballot.[75] These elections were held under careful government supervision during 1979–81. In only a handful of electoral districts are the contests known to have raised important political issues or generated intense contests.[76]

The atmosphere of "democratic reform" under Deng Xiaoping was also reflected in the active roles played by deputies at the third session of the Fifth NPC in September 1980 in criticizing government agencies and raising proposals for improvement.[77]

On the question of constitutional interpretation the 1978 text broke no new ground. The NPC could both amend and "supervise the enforcement of" the constitution; its standing committee could interpret the constitution; the local people's congresses were to safeguard the people's rights and enforce the constitution. Although the 1978 text followed that of 1975 in failing to provide for an independent judiciary, it did restore the procuracy (absent from the 1975 text) and charged the Supreme People's Procuratorate with ensuring observance of the constitution and the law by all organs of state. But the procuracy organic law enacted the following year did not provide any specific powers for discharging this function.[78]

The 1982 Constitution

The 1982 revision was introduced with fanfare as a decisive break with the recent past and a return to the spirit of the 1954 constitution.[79] The Deng Xiaoping group was now in firm command. The new constitution's preamble identified the chief task of the era as economic construction. Class struggle was acknowledged but placed in a subsidiary position. Although the preamble noted the leading role of the Chinese Communist Party and of Marxism-Leninism—Mao Zedong Thought, no substantive article granted the CCP a direct right of rule over any state organ. The vice chairman of the constitutional revision committee, Peng Zhen, explained that his committee had revived the distinction between the Party as a proletarian vanguard organization and the state as an apparatus representing the will of all the classes of the people. The Party should lead but not usurp the role of the state: "The opinions of the Party and people can only become laws and the will of the state when adopted and decided by the National

People's Congress or its Standing Committee. . . . In China, the Constitution and laws are a unity of the stand of the Party and the will of the people."[80]

In the realm of political rights, however, the 1982 draft did not make major departures. Some legal specialists had advocated abandoning the distinction between "people" and "citizens" that dated to the Jiangxi Program,[81] but their suggestions were rejected. The people were still defined as the working class in alliance with the peasants (elucidated by Peng Zhen to include the majority of the intellectuals).[82] A class-free concept of "the people" could not be adopted so long as the leaders believed that, as the preamble put it, "class struggle will continue to exist within certain limits for a long time to come." Article 1 suggested that class struggle was declining in sharpness by defining the state as a "people's democractic dictatorship" rather than 1975's and 1978's "dictatorship of the proletariat," but as if to fend off charges of ideological backsliding, the preamble defined the two terms as synonymous.

Like the three preceding PRC constitutions, the 1982 text mentioned the supression of counterrevolution. But for the first time it did not deprive all persons with bad class backgrounds of their rights, stating only that "the state . . . suppresses treasonable and other counterrevolutionary activities." It restored provisions of the 1954 text that "all citizens . . . are equal before the law" and that the rights to vote and stand for office are enjoyed by citizens without regard to (among other things) distinctions of class background (*jiating chengfen*). All this reflected the fact that the rehabilitation campaign since 1977 had restored most people with bad class backgrounds or political labels to the ranks of the people. However, article 34 did retain the provision that citizens could be deprived of political rights according to law. This left room for the continued banning of the few remaining unreformed landlords, rich peasants, and bureaucratic capitalists as well as for the application of the political deprivation provisions of the 1979 criminal code. In introducing the constitution to the NPC Peng Zhen stated that 99.97 percent of the voting-age citizens enjoyed the right to vote.[83] The remaining quarter-million or so citizens presumably comprised the mentally ill and those deprived of political rights.

For the first time in a PRC constitution, the chapter on rights was placed near the front of the text. Official commentary stressed that this change was meant to symbolize a higher priority for rights.[84] Like its predecessors, the 1982 constitution restored, strengthened, or created some political rights and dropped others. The right to privacy of correspondence was restored—"except . . . in accordance with procedures prescribed by law." The right to strike was dropped. The "four great freedoms" which had been deleted from the 1978 constitution by amendment in 1980 were left out. As in 1954 and 1978, the state organs were obligated in general to "accept supervision" from the people. Both state and collective enterprises were required to involve the workers in management through such devices as workers' and staff congresses, election of managerial staff, or meetings of the entire work force. The article providing for citizen's appeal was both broader and narrower than in 1978. The citizen could "criticize and make suggestions to any state organ or functionary" and could lodge "complaints, charges, or exposures" concerning "violation of law or dereliction of duty by any state organ or functionary." The state was obligated to investigate such complaints. But the drafters did not adopt the suggestion of some scholars that a special administrative court be established to consider citizen complaints, replacing the standard and not very effective practice of referring complaints to superior administrative organs within the same part of the bureaucracy.[85] The new constitution did, however, restore from the 1954 constitution the right of compensation for loss suffered through infringement of rights by the actions of state employees.

The constitution repeated the 1978 provision for the right of citizens to engage in "scientific research, literary and artistic creation, and other cultural pursuits." But it also increased the state's power to enforce ideological orthodoxy. It expanded 1978's three articles on state control of culture to five and took upon the state the responsibility to educate the people in "patriotism, collectivism, internationalism, and communism." It did not repeat the 1978 requirement for citizens to support the leadership of the Communist Party whether they were Party members or not. But the "four basic principles" of ideological orthodoxy (Communist Party leadership, socialism, the dictatorship of the proletariat, and Marxism-Leninism—Mao Zedong Thought) were affirmed in the preamble.[86] Disruption of the socialist system and of the social and economic order were outlawed.

The state's power to limit rights by law was mentioned in one or two articles, not as a general principle. Yet this principle unquestionably underlay this constitution, as all previous Chinese constitutions. Some legal scholars had urged that the 1982 draft break new ground by specifying the principles that the state's limitation of individual rights must satisfy.[87] But the suggestion was not adopted. The rule continued to be that the state could limit rights for any purpose as long as it did so by law.

Perhaps the most substantial change in the area of political rights concerned the rights of national minorities. The 1982 constitution restored and enlarged national minority rights that had been listed in 1954 and condensed or deleted in 1975 and 1978 (see table 2). The government had long recognized fifty-five such minorities, and those living in substantial concentrations had their own regional, prefectural, or county governments. Now the minorities were guaranteed "appropriate" representation in the NPC and its standing committee; they were to have local heads of government of their own races; the local language was to be used in administration and in court proceedings; minority units of government were to be granted limited "autonomous" powers over legislation, finance, economic development, cultural policy, and public security (provisions further spelled out in the 1984 Regional Autonomy Law for Minority Nationalities).[88] But the central government retained ample power to impose coordination and uniformity and to protect national security. The Jiangxi Program's right of minority secession was not repeated.

The new constitution retained the people's congress system and added provisions consistent with the 1979 congressional organic and election laws. It mandated direct election of

Table 2. National Minority Political Rights in PRC Constitutions

	1954	1975	1978	1982
Equality of nationalities	3	4	4	4
Prohibition of discrimination and oppression	3	0	4	4
Use of own language, customs	3	language, 4	4	4
Appropriate representation in NPC	implicit, 2, 3	0	0	59
Appropriate representation in NPC standing committee	0	0	0	65
Local administrative leaders of own nationality	"appropriate representation" 70	0	0	114
Power of local regulation with NPC approval	70	vague, 2, 4	39	116
Power of autonomous finance	70	0	0	117
Independent administration of economic development	0	0	0	118
Independent administration of culture	0	0	0	119
Use of local public security force	70	0	0	120
Use of own language in government	70	0	39	121
Guarantee of state assistance	70	24	40	122
Use of own language in court	77	0	0	134

NOTE: The number in each entry is the article in which the provision appears.

county-level congresses and said that NPC and local people's congress deputies were to be "elected democratically." This shift in language from 1978's "secret ballot after democratic consultation" made room for such new practices as multiple candidates for each post introduced in the 1979 laws. The powers of the people's congresses remained what they had been, though new provisions were introduced to strengthen the ability of standing committees at levels above the county to exercise these powers when congresses were not in session. But other suggestions that had been made to strengthen the role of the people's congresses were not accepted by the drafters of the new constitution—for example, direct election of the NPC, substantial reduction in the NPC's size, extension of the deputies' right to question government beyond the period when the congress was in session, and submission of draft resolutions to deputies in advance of congress sessions.[89]

On the matter of constitutional review and enforcement the 1982 draft held to tradition. "No law or . . . rules and regulations shall contravene the Constitution," stated article 5. But the power to interpret and enforce the constitution and annul contradictory laws did not lie with the courts or procuracy. These were independent but "subject to law," and the new constitution withdrew the 1978 provision giving the procuracy the power to look into whether state organs were operating in accordance with the constitution. The definitive nature of the constitution as a basic law could be enforced only by the supreme legislature and its standing committee—in theory striking down laws it had passed itself, or annulling acts of the administration.

Conclusion: The Chinese Constitutional Tradition and an American Comparison

Chinese constitutions varied widely in eighty years. One constitution was monarchical, the rest republican. The early republican constitutions envisioned competitive politics; those written under Guomindang and Communist auspices allowed a single party to dominate the government. The relations between the president and the cabinet, the executive and the legislature, the center and the provinces changed from one era to the next. As the regime moved from monarchical to republican, from multiparty to single-party, and from Nationalist to Communist, different guiding ideologies were placed in the constitution and different institutions established.

Political rights changed, too. As summarized in table 1, all constitutions granted a common core of political rights consisting of speech, publication, assembly, and association. The rights of petition/appeal, voting, and popular sovereignty were virtually universal. But the right to serve in office and/or sit for the official examination was limited to pre-Communist constitutions; the right of election/recall/initiative/referendum was predominantly a feature of Guomindang constitutions; and rights of procession and demonstration, national minority autonomy, political asylum, supervision of production, supervision of state organs, the "four great freedoms," and the right to strike were limited to Communist constitutions, although not found in all of them. The concept of residual rights was found in three constitutions, all pre-Communist; the right to compensation also appeared in three constitutions, one of them pre-Communist. Several rights were provided in only one constitution each: teaching and study, participation in armed revolution, national minority self-determination, and rights for foreign nationals.

Despite their differences, the series of constitutions established a powerful tradition of continuity with respect to the basic nature of rights. First, in none of the constitutions were rights considered to be derived from human personhood; they were derived from citizenship in the state or, in the case of political rights in the Communist period, from membership in the progressive classes known collectively as "the people." Second, the very variability of rights from constitution to constitution was an important point of continuity. Chinese constitution writers felt able to add and withdraw rights fairly freely because they held that rights are granted by the state and can be changed by the state. Third, some rights in each Chinese constitution were programmatic—that is, they were presented as goals to be realized. This feature was fundamental to the Qing Constitutional Principles, the Guomindang's Tutelage Constitution, and the Communist constitutions, all of which were explicitly written as political programs. And in all the constitutions the feature was implicit in the fact that rights were mentioned which in fact could not be enjoyed.

Fourth, every Chinese constitution implicitly or explicitly gave the government the power to limit rights by acts of legislation. The protection that rights offered lay in the fact that they could not be restricted except by law, not in their forming a limit to law. Fifth, and consequent to the fourth point, none of the constitutions established an effective procedure for independent review of a law's constitutionality. The organ that made the law—emperor, parliament, ruling party, or people's congress—was considered to have the sovereign power to do so, and could not be checked by any other branch of government. Although means were provided for the citizen to appeal against the acts of individual bureaucrats, no avenue was open for the citizen to defend private interests against the laws and policies of the state. The chief goals of all the constitutions were to strengthen the state and promote collective welfare, rather than to protect individual interests against excessive state power.

Sixth, while all but the Qing constitution recognized popular sovereignty in principle, none provided for its effective exercise by the people. In no constitution was the executive directly elected. The national legislature was always elected either indirectly or by a limited electorate and had very limited authority in government affairs. The influence of the citizen over state policy was so buffered and checked as to be negligible in practice.

The meaning of these six points can be sharpened by comparing them to analogous aspects of the American tradition. Such a comparison does not tag the Chinese constitutional tradition as deviant. In fact, there was nothing particularly exotic about the Chinese constitutions. The Qing Principles followed the example of the nearly contemporary Japanese Meiji Constitution;[90] the early republican texts drew on European and American ideas; and the Communist charters were influenced by the Soviet example, especially the Stalin constitution of 1936. The American Constitution is far more unusual by world standards. But for just this reason an American comparison rather than one with the Soviet or Japanese tradition may help best to highlight what was characteristic and consistent in Chinese constitutions over the course of eight decades.

Although American thinking about rights has been diverse and the concept of rights in the American Constitution has changed over the course of two centuries, a central tradition is not hard to find.[91] First, although rights are codified by the state, they are not considered to originate in the state's grant but to be inherent in the dignity or personhood of the individual—some say they are "natural." Second, since rights are seen as discovered rather than enacted, changes in their content are considered to arise from a changing understanding of what is necessary to secure the dignity of the person, not from the changing needs or goals of the state. Once rights are recognized, they are unlikely to be withdrawn. Third, rights are claimed and exercised in the present. They are not goals for the future and cannot be legitimately withheld because conditions are not ripe. Fourth, rights limit legislation rather than vice versa. The exercise of rights is constrained by considerations of other persons' rights and of the public good, but to be enacted into law limits on rights must meet stringent political and legal standards. Public opinion and watchdog groups make it hard for laws limiting rights to be enacted. When challenged in courts, such laws have to be shown to serve clear and compelling state interests, or they are likely to be thrown out. Fifth, an organ independent of the legislature and the executive is empowered to enforce the superiority of the Constitution to other law by testing laws against the standard of the Constitution. Finally, in the American system citizens have effective mechanisms to influence the selection of state personnel and policies. Because of this, political rights have been used by citizens to make demands on government. The freedoms of the press, demonstration, and association and the enforcing power of the vote have helped to protect rights from encroachment and, in fact, to expand them.

In short, the American constitutional tradition sees government, however necessary, as partly an adversary of the individual. The power of the state is constitutionally limited in order to protect individual interests against invasion. The individual has recourse to appeal on behalf of frankly selfish interests not only against bureaucrats who act in disregard of state policy but against state law and policy itself. By contrast, Chinese constitutions assumed a harmony of interests between state and citizen. They did not encourage or even recognize the possibility of conflict between the two. For them the purpose of citizen participation was to mobilize popular energies to serve the state. What served the state's interests served the citizen's. Although means were provided for the citizen to appeal against the acts of individual bureaucrats, no avenue was open in any Chinese constitution for the citizen to defend private interests against laws and policies of the state that might damage them.

The idea that China should have a constitution and that the constitution should specify individual rights came from abroad. But constitutions and rights came to be understood in Chinese terms—terms selected from among the points of view available in the tradition, then altered and refined in a process of internal debate among participants who drew on contemporary world trends of thought, including Marxism. Though many aspects of the dominant rights ideology remain controversial in China, the fact that the eleven major constitutions and drafts of this century had so much in common gives good reason to believe that they reflected fundamental cultural values, shared by the successive political elites who wrote them over the course of eight decades of ideological turmoil and political revolution. The exploration of these central themes of the Chinese rights tradition forms the subject of the fourth essay.

4.

Sources of Chinese Rights Thinking

Andrew J. Nathan

*I*n any modern nation, constitutional and legal provisions for political rights define how the citizen can
legitimately attempt to influence government. In the eight decades
of China's history as a constitutional nation, no constitution has
remained in effect for very long, and none has been fully obeyed
by the regime that promulgated it. Yet the constitutions embodied
the negotiated consensus of dominant groups in society about what
they considered the proper political relations between citizens and
the state. As shown in essay 3, the eleven constitutions and major
drafts all treated political rights as grants given by the state to the
citizen to enable him to contribute his energies to the needs of the
nation.

The eleven texts represented the thinking of four very
different regimes; the political rights that they granted varied as
well, except for a common core consisting of the rights of speech,
publication, assembly, and association (see table 1, in essay 3).
Yet a tradition of rights thinking emerged in the series of texts. Its
six identifying characteristics were that it derived rights from citizenship or membership in the people rather than from human
personhood as such; that it permitted considerable variability in

the content of rights from constitution to constitution in light of the changing needs of the state; that it treated some rights as programmatic goals rather than as immediate claims on government; that it gave the government the power to limit rights by acts of legislation; that it did not establish effective means of independent review of the constitutionality of laws; and that it did not provide for the effective exercise of popular sovereignty. I suggested in the third essay that the values underlying these six features could be better understood by looking at how the Chinese constitutional tradition emerged out of the confrontation of time-honored ideas with modern national needs and imported political and legal concepts. This essay explores four such themes in Chinese thinking about rights: ideas about the proper scope of state power and the nature of law; conceptions of the relationship between individual and collective interests; beliefs about what the state owes its people and what it expects from them; and ideas about the social utility of rights.

Law as the Will of the State

Every constitution implies a conception of the proper powers of the state and the sources and limits of law. The American constitutional tradition, for example, rests on a philosophy of "natural rights," a belief that the proper sphere of state power is limited by moral claims prior to and superior in status to the state's laws. This philosophy is expressed in the Declaration of Independence, in many of the state constitutions that predated the federal Constitution, and in the ten constitutional amendments that form the Bill of Rights. As Louis Henkin has pointed out, the amendments state that various rights "may not be abridged" without defining their content, because these rights were thought to exist and to be known independently of their enactment by the state. The concern of the Bill of Rights was to protect them from invasion, not to define them.[1] Rights have been reinterpreted and enlarged in the subsequent centuries and new ones have been added, but the basic American understanding remains that rights are entitlements founded in the human condition rather than granted by the state.

Chinese thinking about law was shaped by two ancient schools, Legalism and Confucianism.[2] Both accepted the ruler's right to make law. The Legalists viewed this right as unconstrained by any higher moral order. They held that the ruler could and should create any laws necessary to strengthen his state, and that harsh laws worked better than soft ones. The Confucians argued that to be effective, law must comply with the moral order inherent in society. The laws and the ruler must be fair and just and must encourage the virtues of filiality, loyalty, and social compassion. This Confucian view was parallel in a broad sense to the Western concept of natural law in that it believed in a moral order independent of the laws of the state.

For the Confucians, however, this was a moral order created by man, not nature. More important, the moral order the Confucians believed in differed in content from that which underlay modern Western theories of natural law such as those of Hobbes, Locke, and Rousseau. Confucians did not see the moral order as limiting the powers of the ruler. Instead, they saw it as calling for the fulfillment of the ruler's and the people's innate promptings as social beings. To comply with the moral order meant for the ruler to extend his charismatic virtue to the full. As Wm. Theodore deBary puts it, "Moral restraints . . . are intended not to make [the Prince] less of a king but to help him be a king."[3] In particular, the Confucian moral order contained no belief in the rights of the individual as a limit on any kind of authority—including that of the clan, family, parents, or husbands. So while the Chinese tradition like any other had its own sense of what was naturally right, neither Legalism nor Confucianism saw moral laws or individual rights as limiting the power of the state.

At the time that Chinese thinkers began to look abroad for guidance in modernizing the legal system, they found the idea of natural rights wrapped in what was to them a particularly mystifying guise, social contract theory. Hobbes and Rousseau were introduced to Chinese readers by the influential late Qing journalist and politician Liang Qichao (1873–1929). Liang treated the notion that man had ever existed outside of society in a state of nature as a curiosity. He expressed shock at the primitive morality of Hobbes' vision of the war of each against all. He did not seem aware that it was a basic premise of both writers that the individual had interests separate from those of society.[4] Liang was far more comfortable with the ideas of Johann Kaspar Bluntschli, a Swiss political scientist whose works he had discovered through Japanese translations. Bluntschli argued that the state is not merely an aggregation of individuals but an organic entity. This proved to Liang that the individual's status as a citizen and therefore his rights derive from the state, not the other way around.[5]

At the time that Liang wrote—a few years before the drafting of the Principles of the Constitution—natural rights ideas were in retreat in the West. European and American legal theorists were increasingly influenced by the doctrine of legal positivism developed by the nineteenth-century English theorist, John Austin (1790–1859). According to Austin, the so-called laws of God, nature, or morality are just expressions of philosophers' preferences, dressed up with the claim to be law. Properly speaking, laws are whatever commands are enacted by a political sovereign and backed up with the threat of punishment. This theory could be taken in diverse directions. It was associated in Britain with the liberal reform philosophy of utilitarianism and in America with the school of "legal realism" which directed attention to the factors that influence the actual behavior of courts. But in Germany, Italy, and the Soviet Union, legal positivism combined with doctrines of the absolute state to help provide the ideological foundation for fascism and Stalinism.[6]

In China, too, beginning in the late nineteenth century, the theory of legal positivism was put to the service of creating a strong state. With increasing urgency after 1895, the Chinese were searching abroad for methods of strengthening their government. The study of foreign legal theory was part of this quest. Before the

Principles of the Constitution were drafted the imperial court sent two groups of commissioners overseas to study constitutional models. The tours resulted in lengthy compilations built around the theme of how constitutions augmented the power of the state in Europe and Japan.[7] When the Principles were submitted to the Empress Dowager, they were accompanied with the following summary of their spirit:

First, the sacred majesty of the sovereign may not be offended against. Second, the sovereign has absolute power, which he exercises in constitutional forms. Third, the [subjects], according to the laws, have privileges to which they are entitled and duties which they owe.[8]

As the century wore on, returned students dominated the university law schools, comparative government faculties, and legal drafting commissions of successive governments. Because of linguistic and geographic convenience, the Japanese influence was particularly strong; Germany also exerted considerable influence both directly and through Japan. The jurisprudence of both countries was based on the doctrine of legal positivism. One scholar of the Guomindang period summarized the then accepted view of law and rights as follows:

It must be realized at the outset that constitutional rights should not be based on the theory of natural rights. It is beyond controversy that any enforceable right is the creation of the law. Only when the law recognizes a certain right is such a right legally protected. It naturally follows that the law may make the right and also may unmake it. Constitutional right as a form of legal right is no exception.[9]

This view of rights was so dominant that few extended statements of the competing natural rights theory were offered in China. Perhaps the most influential such work was *Freedom and Human Rights*, published in 1954 by political philosopher Zhang Foquan in Taiwan.[10] Zhang contended that human rights are inalienable and do not depend upon the power of the state. But to make this case he had to rely almost entirely on Western authorities, especially Locke, tacitly acknowledging the lack of support for his position in the native legal tradition. He did not even mention the application of his theory to China until the next-to-last chapter of his book, where he observed that the idea of natural rights was as yet little understood among his countrymen. He advocated adding to the 1946 constitution then in effect in Taiwan a "proper" Bill of Rights that recognized the primacy of individual rights over state power. This step, of course, was never taken.

On the mainland, meanwhile, legal positivism took Marxist shape as the theory that law is the will of the ruling class expressed in fixed form. As explained by the official party journal, *Red Flag*, "In a class society, only after obtaining political power can the ruling class, by means of the form of law, transform the will of its own class into the will of the state, and rely on the state's coercive force to safeguard its own class interests."[11] So far as the theory of rights was concerned this did not involve a major shift. Like the Guomindang, the Communists rejected the concept of fixed and universal "human rights." Again in the words of *Red Flag*, "Human rights are not 'heaven-given,' they are given and regulated by the state and by law; they are not universal, but have a clear class nature; they are not abstract but concrete; they are not absolute but limited by law and morality; they are not eternally fixed and unchanging but change their nature and proper scope in accordance with changes in the functions and position of people in the midst of shifting conditions of material production." Thus the Communist state recognizes only "civil" (or "citizens' ") rights, created by the state and granted to its citizens. "The content of civil rights may not be completely identical [even] among countries with the same political systems, because the civil rights are specifically stipulated by each country's own constitution."[12]

In short, Chinese predispositions and foreign influences combined to forge a philosophy of law as the state's will and rights as the state's creation. This philosophy, in turn, helps explain several characteristics of Chinese constitutions. First, if rights are created by the state, it is reasonable for rights provisions to be programmatic. The constitution need not list preexisting limits on state powers, but can announce what rights the state hopes to provide in due course, without embarrassment that the rights are not yet available. Second, it is reasonable for the state to grant rights only to those who are friendly or loyal to it or who are its "members," and to deprive of their enjoyment those who are hostile to its purposes. As the *Workers' Daily* put it with respect to freedom of speech, this "is not an innate right which can be exploited even after the proletariat succeeds in seizing power. . . . In order to protect socialist public ownership and consolidate its political rule, the proletariat must give political rights and freedoms, including freedom of speech, to the masses instead of to the antagonistic classes or their remnants."[13]

      Third, since the state creates rights, it is reasonable that it has full powers to restrict them, so long as it does so in the same way that it grants them—by legislative enactment. As the chief drafter of the 1946 constitution, John C. H. Wu, put it: "Rights are entrusted by society to the individual; society is the source of rights. The individual apart from society has no rights to speak of. Since society bestows rights, at times of necessity it can also remove rights; at least it can limit their scope."[14] Or as explained in the Chinese journal *Democracy and the Legal System*, "The state has the right to intervene in all civil activities which run counter to state planning and state laws and decrees."[15] Fourth, since the state acts legitimately when it restricts rights by law, no law can be invalid merely because it restricts rights so long as it is a properly enacted law, and no procedure is needed to determine whether particular laws do violate rights. In a recent example, when the members of China's small Democracy Movement (1978–81) tried to defend their right to publish private mimeographed periodicals on the basis of constitutional guarantees of freedom of speech and publication, there was no institution with which to lodge their appeal except the same police precincts that were closing them down.[16]

      Some Chinese political leaders have stretched the idea of the unfettered state to justify acts that many legal theorists, Chinese and Western alike, would not accept. Modern legal theories, including Marxism, generally make a distinction between the decisions of the ruler or the ruling party and the laws of the state. The word "state" is reserved for the sovereign authority and the word "law" for the general rules that it commands its subjects to obey. In these theories, to say that rights may be restricted by law means that they can be restricted only by enacting general rules through the formal procedures of state legislative organs, not by setting policies of the ruling party or by issuing orders reflecting the case-by-case preferences of officials. But Chinese constitution writers have not always kept these distinctions clear. In the 1908 Qing Principles, for example, the emperor undertook not to restrict rights except by law, but at the same time preserved the tradition of personal rule by retaining for himself the full power to make law. The 1931 Tutelage Constitution recognized that only law could restrict rights, but gave the ruling party unlimited power to appoint officers of the state and to interpret law and the constitution. The 1975 constitution made the National People's Congress subject to the leadership of the Communist Party.

What constitutions sometimes obscured, people in power often ignored. For example, until very recently the Communist Party has held that it can legitimately restrict rights through its own decisions or policies rather than only through state law. For at least two decades beginning in the late 1950s, Party policies were therefore held to have the same effect as law. "We work according to party policies and the interests of the people," a legal official told a foreign journalist in 1974. "There is in the country now no published code but we have individual regulations concerning penalties against counterrevolutionaries. If the case is not covered by one of the special regulations we deal with it according to the policy of the party."[17] Under this system tens of thousands of persons were punished for violating Party regulations or policies they did not know existed, or for acts that were judged culpable by local Party leaders. Verdicts and sentences were decided in batches by Party officials in camera.[18]

In 1984 the chairman of the Standing Committee of the National People's Congress, Peng Zhen, stated, "we must gradually make the transition from relying on policy in managing affairs, to establishing and strengthening the legal system and relying not only on policy but also on law to manage affairs."[19] The legal reforms of the 1980s have accordingly returned the responsibility of decision in criminal cases to the courts, where verdicts and sentences are supposed to be based on enacted laws. In interpreting and applying the law, however, judges are still required to be guided by Party policy.[20] According to one commentator, "The party's policies for the life of the state are accepted by state organs as the policies of the state . . . [and] do, in fact, play the role of law."[21] A 1981 college law text states: "Legislation must take party policy as its basis, and administration of the law must take party policy as its guide. When legal provisions are lacking, we should manage affairs in accordance with party policy. When legal provisions exist they should be accurately applied, also under the guidance of party policy. . . . Policy occupies the leading position. . . . Law serves to bring policy to fruition."[22]

A second stretching of the notion that law is the state's will occurred on several occasions when the authorities suspended rights—either for limited numbers of persons or for the whole population—without following legal procedures for doing so. One such instance was the Nationalist Government's imposition of martial law in Taiwan in 1949. The 1946 constitution had provided that the president could declare martial law with the concurrence of the Legislative Yuan. But in 1948, because an emergency existed and the Legislative Yuan was not in session, the National Assembly (a separate organ) granted the president power to take emergency measures without going through the constitutional procedures. Then, when a state of siege was actually declared in Taiwan in 1949, it was done not by the president but by a unit of the military. Under this constitutionally questionable state of siege, still in effect today in Taiwan, the scope of political offenses has been broadened, their penalties increased, and military courts have taken jurisdiction over them.[23]

The procedure for suspending rights during the Cultural Revolution was even less orderly. People were persecuted by ad hoc authorities through nonlegal procedures for acts that were deemed political crimes on no legal basis. The head of state, Liu

Shaoqi, was deposed without action of the National's People's Congress and imprisoned without a criminal charge or a trial. All this was officially defended at the time as "revolutionary legality" required for class struggle. As recently as 1980, the newly enacted criminal and criminal procedure laws were disregarded in the "trial of the Gang of Four and Lin Biao counterrevolutionary cliques."[24] In this case the irregularities were explained on the grounds of the extraordinary nature of the case.

Like the idea of the legal force of Party policy, the notion that rights can be suspended by extralegal procedures has been controversial. During the discussion of the 1982 draft constitution at least one scholar urged that strict procedures be established for suspending the constitution in case of need.[25] The idea was only partially accepted: the NPC Standing Committee was given the power to declare martial law (a provision also found in the 1954 constitution). In fact, there is evidence that many Chinese still doubt that the Party leaders will honor the constitution in a crisis.[26]

Propelled to some extent by the lobbying of Chinese lawyers, the idea of the supremacy of law is being reemphasized and may eventually become an entrenched part of the evolving Chinese concept of rights. If this happens, the limits of rights may become more clearly defined. But they will not necessarily be significantly widened. That would depend upon the particular concept of rights embodied in the laws enacted to define them. And judging from recent legislation and the manner of its enforcement by the government, that concept remains tightly bounded by the interests of the state.

For example, three laws now define the scope of one of the most important political rights, freedom of speech. First, the constitution establishes an obligation for each citizen to uphold the "four basic principles"—Party leadership, socialism, dictatorship of the proletariat, and Marxism-Leninism—Mao Zedong Thought. Second, the state secrets regulations of 1951 prohibit the revelation of matters which are classified as secrets of state or which "ought not be revealed." Finally, the 1979 criminal code contains a number of articles restricting acts of speech, such as those instigating others to crime, lodging false charges, making libelous statements, or making false identification or appraisal. The most important speech-related provision of the criminal code is article 102, which classifies counterrevolutionary incitement or propaganda as crimes punishable by imprisonment of at least five years' duration. The code defines counterrevolutionary offenses as "acts undertaken with the purpose of overthrowing the political power of the dictatorship of the proletariat and the socialist system and which harm the Chinese People's Republic."[27] In principle, thus, counterrevolutionary crimes require an intention, an act, and a harmful consequence.[28] But in the cases of Wei Jingsheng and other Democracy Movement activists in 1979–81, the mere posting or mimeographing of critical essays or the dropping of leaflets was punished as counterrevolutionary incitement even though there was no explicit call for the overthrow of the regime, no inciting act beyond dissemination of written material, and no measurable damage done to the state.[29] Summarizing the legal provisions pertaining to speech, *Red Flag* pointed out: "A person is free to express any opinion (including erroneous ones) and will be protected by law so long as he stands on the side of the people and safeguards the constitution and the law. . . . [But] no one is allowed to air antiparty and antisocialist views."[30]

Under the laws, conversation, academic discourse, and correspondence can all be punished if their content is objectionable. As one newspaper article explained, "Speech takes place; it enters the realm of reality and there is the possibility that it may attach itself to certain kinds of conduct."[31] So far the only act of speech unambiguously designated as exempt from prosecution is writing in a diary, so long as no steps are taken to disseminate the ideas. Yet diary entries have been used as evidence of counterrevolutionary intent, thus making serious crimes out of acts that would otherwise have been punished less severely or not at all.[32] A number of Chinese journal articles have argued the need for further legal protection for free speech. In the words of one of them, "As long as the principle that 'speech is no crime' continues to be a kind of political principle without a legal guarantee as in the past, then the citizen's right of free speech cannot be fully protected, people's fear of being punished for speech cannot be extinguished, and the tragedy of 'literary crimes' can still occur. For if [freedom of speech] is indeed a 'political principle' then it may depend on the political atmosphere, the character and attitudes of political personalities and similar factors to determine whether it can be exercised or not and if so to what degree."[33]

In the current state of Chinese law, other political rights are equally narrowly restricted. The rights of assembly and association, procession and demonstration are restricted by both constitutional and criminal provisions against damaging public order, interfering with traffic, disrupting work, harming social morals, and damaging state property. Officials have treated almost all demonstrations and unauthorized public meetings as if they were in violation of these restrictions, and have sometimes called them counterrevolutionary besides.[34] The right to petition and appeal has been narrowed in the same way. Appeals that are importunate, persistent, or "unreasonable" in content are punishable as counterrevolutionary incitement or violations of public order or are punished by work unit officials or the police as ideological deviations.[35] The right to publication is governed by the outdated publications regulations which set conditions private publications cannot meet and by the state secrets regulations which classify state secrets broadly enough to include any state matter not already officially published (a new press law is reportedly in preparation).[36]

Moreover, in practice, the difficult constitutional and philosophical issues of the permissible boundaries of the exercise of all these rights have often been left for resolution to the police rather than to the legislature or the courts. Under the 1957 regulations on rehabilitation through labor the police may sentence to renewable terms of three years' service in a labor camp "counterrevolutionaries and antisocialist reactionaries who, because their crimes are minor, are not pursued for criminal responsibility"— i.e., who are not given court trials.[37] Chinese press reports suggest that most political dissidents have been dealt with in this way, including some fifty or more Democracy Movement activists arrested in 1979–81.[38]

As the role of law increases in Chinese society, rights are better defined and protected than they were, for example, in the late 1960s and early 1970s, when people were given long prison terms for such minor acts as accidently defacing Mao's picture.[39] But so far, the state's power to restrict rights by law continues to be used in such a way as to define each right's boundaries narrowly, and to leave the individual little opportunity to challenge official interpretations of these boundaries.

Unselfish Individualism and Higher Interests

The strong state did not collide in China with the kind of individualism that might have offered a bulwark against extensive use of its legal power to restrict rights, as had been the case, for example, in England, where parliamentary supremacy was checked by the forces of common law and public opinion. There was, to be sure, a Chinese tradition of the unusual individual divorcing himself from politics to seek religious or artistic insight. But those who took this path did not do so in order to serve as a check on the state, but simply to escape from the normal political obligations of their class. For those who remained in society, Chinese philosophy still assigned a great role to individuals, but this was a political individualism of a very different kind from that which the term calls to mind in the modern West.

Western philosophers since the seventeenth century have assumed that the individual has interests of his own that are distinct from those of society. A leading problem has been how to reconcile these two kinds of interest. Some thinkers argued that the individual's interests are served by society, others that society's interests are served by the self-interested activity of individuals, and still others that the conflict could be compromised by limiting both government's power to coerce the individual and the individual's power to benefit himself at the expense of others. In any case, it was generally agreed that the individual had a right to do as much for himself as he could without invading the rights of others, and that to justify themselves society and government must offer some benefit to the individual. In short, modern Western philosophy has seen individual interests as both real and legitimate.

Confucianism recognized the existence of private interests in society, but it viewed them as belonging not to the individual but to the group—a family, lineage, or community. In the Confucian view, man is born into society and cannot prosper alone; the individual depends on the harmony and strength of the group. Selfish behavior was viewed as reflecting, in Donald Munro's words, "a failure to perceive oneself in terms of a more comprehensive entity to which one belongs and a futile attempt to isolate oneself from it."[40] Ethically, in the words of Hsieh Yu-Wei, Confucianism "regarded individuals as roots, and communities as leaves—or individuals as foundations and communities as roofs."[41] The individual must cultivate himself, not for himself, but so that he can contribute to the welfare of family and community. As Derk Bodde has pointed out, "Confucian individualism" means that the individual must develop his creative potentialities so that he can fulfill "that particular role which is his within the social nexus."[42]

The selfish "small man" had neither the power nor the right to influence events. By contrast, the "great man" (junzi) had immense power to change the world. Such a person was an individualist in the sense that he followed his own moral beliefs. But a true great man was never motivated by selfish ends: lack of selfish interests was the very source of his power of moral suasion. Confucian heroes were men like Qu Yuan, who dared to remonstrate with his prince and willingly accepted the penalty of exile; Liu Yin, who withdrew to the straitened life of a teacher rather than serve in office in a degenerate age; and Wang Yangming, who struggled to reach a personal reformulation of the Confucian ideal of sagehood.[43] They followed their personal visions of the truth, not in order to aggrandize themselves but to affirm morality and serve society. Those who dared to remonstrate with the ruler were admired for their honesty and courage, but they neither enjoyed nor expected legal protection from punishment. In the most celebrated cases, their individualism led to personal sacrifice rather than enrichment.

The Confucian critique of despotism likewise reflected the assumption of the primacy of the community. The thinkers who developed this critique most fully were Huang Zongxi, Gu Yanwu, and Wang Fuzhi, none of whom criticized tyranny because it deprived men of the property or freedom that should be theirs. All argued that despotism harmed the social order and the regime itself by crushing the impulse of subjects, especially the literati, to serve the ruler in a morally self-directed, creative way. When Huang Zongxi, perhaps the most daring of these thinkers, challenged the legitimacy of dynastic rule, he did so on the grounds that the Ming emperors had exalted the private interests of the ruling house over the public interests of the community.[44]

It was against this background that modern Chinese thinkers confronted Western ideas of self-interested individualism. One of the earlier attempts to wrestle with this aspect of Western thought was Liang Qichao's 1896 essay "The Sources of China's Weakness Lie in Restrictions Intended to Prevent Abuses." Liang argued that unlike China, Western countries were strong because their citizens had rights. He explained this by defining rights not as claims against society but as the power to do within society "that which it is appropriate to do, and to enjoy the benefits that are owing to one." If all citizens exercise this kind of power, the state will be powerful as well:

[For] a state consists of an accumulation of powers. A state with a full panoply of powers is strong; one with few powers is in difficulties; one without powers is lost. By a full panoply of powers I mean the situation where each individual exercises his own power."[45]

Here Liang did not envision that rights granted to the individual might be used in ways contrary to the interests of the state. The conflict so important in Western thought did not exist in his account. Approaching the subject from the other end, Liang also did not worry that a strengthened state might threaten the interests of individuals:

The individual cannot survive alone in the world. Society thus arises,

and the individual manages his existence in collaboration with his fellows.
. . . One who is good at pursuing his own interests will first see to the
interests of his collectivity, and then his own interests will be advanced
along with it.[46]

Indeed, the identity of individual and collective interests was even
more compelling now than in earlier times, in Liang's view, because the survival of the Chinese race was at stake. The white race
had already overwhelmed five of the six continents and was gath-
ering its forces for an assault on China.[47] With the famous trans-
lator, Yan Fu, Liang taught a generation about the new science of
Darwinism that showed how, according to them, the individual
might perish but his interests were served if his race survived.[48]

      The early decades of this century were years of liber-
ation for Chinese intellectuals. Iconoclasm flourished. Confucian
social duties were challenged by young rebels. No school of thought,
including the most individualistic, lacked its handful of believers.
Yet it is hard to find even among the Chinese anarchists, Ibsenites,
and Nietzscheans a consistent defender of self-interested individualism. The impulse was too strong to defend liberation as serving
society. For example, the anarchist Liu Shipei wrote that "we stand
for . . . uniting all the people of the world into one great mass to
plan the complete happiness of mankind."[49] The liberal scholar
Hu Shi introduced Ibsen's slogan "Save yourself" with the defense
that "such egoism is in fact the most valuable kind of altruism.
. . . If society and the nation do not possess [men of] independent
character, they are like wine without yeast, bread without leaven,
the human body without nerves. Such a society has absolutely no
hope of improvement or progress.[50] Chen Duxiu's famous 1915
essay "Call to Youth" cited Nietzsche in calling on Chinese youth
to shake off the Confucian "slavish morality" and become "completely independent and free personalities" because, said Chen,
"I would much rather see the past culture of our nation disappear
than see our race die out now because of its unfitness for living in
the modern world."[51] Guo Moruo, a Chinese disciple of Nietzsche,
Goethe, Carlyle, and Whitman who wrote a poem with the line
"My ego is about to burst," also wrote soon afterward that "the
minority who are far-sighted should sacrifice their own individ-

uality, sacrifice their own freedom to save the masses, to reclaim the individuality and freedom of the great mass of the people."[52] As heirs to the literati tradition of social service, and as citizens of a threatened nation, modern Chinese intellectuals could not justify the liberation of the individual on the frankly selfish grounds so often employed in the modern West.

With the arrival of Marxism this ethic of selflessness was preserved in tandem with the Marxian emphasis on material interests. Marx saw the proletariat as compelled by self-interest to liberate mankind, with the workers driven to revolution by hardship and exploitation. Communism creates a society so productive that each individual has access to all the goods he needs and to the leisure to develop fully as a person. Thus the individual material interest of each member of the proletariat is an important goal of socialism, in Marx's view. Chinese Marxism accepts the legitimacy of individual interest but only in a limited sense; it argues that this interest both is, and should be, subordinate to the higher interests of party, class, and nation. Individual and collective interests may sometimes seem to come into conflict, but this conflict is reconcilable. As Mao wrote: "The individual is an element of the collective. When collective interests are increased, personal interests will subsequently be improved."[53] The party therefore leads the people to see that, in the words of a Chinese philosopher, "the benefits of the social collective are more important than individual benefits, long-term benefits are more important than short-term benefits, and complete benefits are more important than partial benefits."[54] "When people struggle for socialism," states *Red Flag*, "they not only are bringing benefits to other people and future generations but are objectively striving for their own immediate and long-term interests."[55] Reviving a Social Darwinist theme of the late Qing thinkers, *Red Flag* even argued in 1983 that "the destiny of the motherland and the destiny of an individual are as inseparable as flesh and blood. One loses one's family if one's country is destroyed. If the motherland is not prosperous and developed, individuals cannot find outlets for their abilities."[56]

In this view, not all individual interests are recognized as legitimate: "The legitimate individual interests that we say should be protected by the party and the nation refer to the individual interests of the worker that are at one with the national and collective benefits."[57] In case of conflict, members of a socialist society should behave selflessly, even to the point of self-sacrifice.

> The spirit of selflessness is a reflection of the essential disposition of the proletariat. Our party . . . demands that both party members and the masses take the selfless spirit as the moral norm of their own words and deeds and make a rupture with bourgeois individualism. Under the nurturing of the party, the vast ranks of party members and the masses all take selflessness as a glory and selfishness as a shame.[58]

"When individual interests and party interests are found to be inconsistent with each other," writes another commentator, "we should be able unhesitatingly and without any reluctance to obey party interests and sacrifice individual interests."[59] A third article adds: "When others are happy, when the people are happy, the purpose of our own freedoms is also realized. Have not our revolutionary predecessors, our hundreds and thousands of martyrs in the past, sacrificed their lives and shed their blood precisely for such freedoms?"[60]

      The ethic of proletarian selflessness still leaves room for the heroic individual, but, as under Confucianism, such a person's goals must be selfless. Former Defense Minister Peng Dehuai, for example, is now considered a hero because he spoke up against Mao's Great Leap policies in 1959 and then accepted his punishment of living out the rest of his life in obscurity. Communist Party member Zhang Zhixin was posthumously lionized for having written to Mao to complain about the "ultraleftist" policies of those around him; she was executed after her throat was slit so she could not shout "Long Live Chairman Mao" at the execution ground.[61] A repairman at a broadcast station, Yue Zengshou, wrote twelve letters to Chairman Mao and other high officials exposing the supposedly model agricultural brigade at Dazhai. "For the sake of pursuing truth," he wrote, "I have risked punishment and death to report this." He was arrested, denounced in a mass meeting, tortured, and sentenced to eighteen years in prison; his relatives were also punished. He was praised in the press after being cleared in 1979.[62] In Jiangxi a husband and wife sent the central authorities twenty-seven articles and letters expressing what were later deemed "correct opinions on a whole series of important issues." The husband was executed in 1970, the wife died the following year in a labor camp. They were held up as models for expressing the following attitude: "We do not fear plunging into boiling water, walking on fire, or having our bodies and bones broken, so long as the great Chinese Communist Party can continue to exist and the great socialist fatherland can develop."[63] What these and similar publicly recognized heroes have in common is that they exercised their rights solely in the public interest and accepted the risk of great personal sacrifice. Also, the substance of their criticisms was judged in retrospect to have been correct; otherwise they might have been rehabilitated but not praised for what they did.[64]

In short, the Confucian understanding of the empirical and ethical relationship between the individual and society continues to inform Chinese political thought in this century—the factual proposition that properly understood the individual's interests are inseparable from those of society, and the ethical injunction to place the interests of society first. These views buttress the Chinese constitutional tradition at several points. First, they give added justification and latitude to the state's power to restrict individual rights. They suggest that the state may properly restrict rights not just for reasons of extreme urgency but in whatever ways serve the interests of society, for in doing so the state is actually serving the higher interests of the individuals who are being restricted. As the PRC journal *Legal Research* explained:

Even some members of the ruling class itself [i.e., the proletariat] must suffer the restraint of law if they clash with the basic interests of their class. . . . Freedom under socialism is freedom which does not contravene the basic interests of the broad masses of the people; it is freedom which respects the social order and which respects necessary discipline.[65]

The individual in turn should recognize such restrictions as serving his higher interests and should embrace them willingly. In the words of Chiang Kai-shek,

We must recognize that an individual can survive and make progress only as a part of a state and a nation. Thus the life of an individual depends upon the life of the state and nation. The authority of the Government should be based on the free and voluntary will of the individual. Moreover, the demands of the state and the nation should become the free and voluntary demands of individuals.[66]

Since one's own rights are tied up with the collective welfare, their selfish exercise on an individual basis would be self-defeating because it would harm the collective interest and hence one's higher interests. On the other hand, full realization of the collective interest would guarantee fulfillment of one's individual rights and freedoms in a higher sense even if one did not exercise them directly oneself.

Second, the ethic of selflessness demands self-restraint in the exercise of individual rights that sometimes goes beyond even the restrictions imposed by law. As *Guangming ribao* explained in 1981, there is a distinction between "legal individual interest" and "legitimate individual interest" (*geren hefa liyi, geren zhengdang liyi*). "Not all individual interests in accord with socialist laws are necessarily morally legitimate," the newspaper argued. "Whether they are legitimate or not depends upon their relation to the collective interests of the society at a given time."[67] Thus the fact that a person has a certain right under the constitution does not make it morally correct to exercise that right to the fullest. Appealing and letter-writing, for example, are protected under both the party and state constitutions, and officials are forbidden to retaliate against those who complain through proper channels. But appeals which demand compensation that the state cannot afford to provide have been ruled "unreasonable" even if the citizen involved has the law on his side.[68] In the realm of speech, "We often emphasize 'not saying anything that is not good for unity,' " according to *Workers' Daily*, "and if anyone publishes this kind of opinion, although he will not be punished by law, he will be criticized and denounced by the opinion of society."[69] An example of this kind of social denunciation was the reaction of the official press to the Democracy Movement. Besides administrative or criminal punishment, much moral invective was directed at the democratic activists and petitioners who tried to exercise the constitutional rights of publication, speech, and petition more aggressively than the authorities deemed suitable. Fu Yuehua, a leader of a group of peasant petitioners in Peking, was not only prosecuted for disturbing the peace but was gratuitously accused of immoral sexual behavior, laziness, theft, and lying.[70] Wei Jingsheng, who was sentenced to fifteen years' imprisonment for counterrevolutionary utterances and betrayal of state secrets, was also accused of fraud, speculation, theft, and being lazy on the job, although he was not prosecuted for these crimes.[71] A handful of workers and students who claimed constitutional protection for their right to publish mimeographed literary and theoretical periodicals were publicly denounced for anarchism and bourgeois individualism as well as being detained by the police for "labor education."

On the other hand, much praise was given during the same period to persons who limited their exercise of individual rights in order to protect the higher interests of the community. For example, drilling instructor Guo Xingfu was lauded in 1980 for returning to work side-by-side with those who had persecuted him during the Cultural Revolution. Guo had reportedly been labeled a "black capable person" (i.e., a nonpolitical technical specialist) in 1967, tortured "for a long time" and imprisoned; all his family except his wife and him were "driven to suicide" and his health and memory were "badly ruined." But upon rehabilitation by the Central Military Commission, Guo "focused his hatred" on the public symbols of Lin Biao and the Gang of Four and did not pursue his rights to compensation or prosecution of his tormentors.[72]

Third, the state and the ruling Party have undertaken to see that the ethic of selflessness is widely understood. In the words of one PRC newspaper, "[Socialist] freedoms can exist and develop only when, under the leadership of the party, we educate and guide the vast ranks of the masses of people by making use of the communist world view and view of life, when we overcome the individualism, departmentalism, and bourgeois view of democracy and freedom that still exist in the thinking of some people, when we establish communist morals and customs."[73] The Tutelage Constitution spoke of education in the Three People's Principles, and the 1946 constitution of the responsibility of educators to inculcate patriotism and civic morality. In the 1982 constitution moral training in selflessness was included as a task of the state: "The state advocates the civic virtues of love for the motherland, for the people, for labor, for science, and for socialism; it educates the people in patriotism, collectivism, internationalism and communism, and in dialectical and historical materialism; it combats capitalist, feudalist, and other decadent ideas." The government has exercised this responsibility in many ways. For example, it conducts an extensive campaign every March to promote "socialist ethics" in China's cities, encouraging people not only to obey the law but also to contribute voluntarily to the collective welfare in ways that go beyond the requirements of the law.

Finally, the concept of higher interests helps clarify why Chinese constitutions since the founding of the republic have recognized popular sovereignty in principle but have not contained provisions to enable citizens actually to influence government personnel or policy. In Guomindang and Chinese Communist theory the ruling party is, respectively, the representative of the nation or the vanguard of the progressive classes. In either case, it has no interests of its own, ruling solely in the interests of the nation and the people. It follows that rule by the Party's leaders is by definition rule in the people's interests and democratic. A commentary on the 1982 constitution explained this line of argument:

In socialist countries, as the people are the masters of the country and the government is the people's government, the subject and object of management are consistent with each other. In other words, the masses of the people are simultaneously conductors and objects of state management. This determines that in the socialist state administrative management bears the nature of a democracy.[74]

In this conception, democracy is a matter of the interests rule serves rather than of procedures for selecting rulers; procedural guarantees of democracy are relatively unimportant. Mao once remarked, "I don't trust elections. . . . I was elected from Peking [to the NPC], but many people have never even seen me! If they haven't seen me how can they vote for me? They've just heard my name."[75] Mao's point was that he claimed to represent the people not because he was elected by them but because he stood for their interests. Chinese analysts argue that the procedural freedom of bourgeois democratic systems is illusory. It allows individual workers and farmers to speak, vote, and lobby without restraint but in the end serves the interests of the bourgeoisie. Because socialist democracy is based on public ownership of the means of production, it serves the people's true interests by definition. "It may not appear as colorful in form as bourgeois democracy, but it is the most extensive and substantial democracy in mankind's history."[76]

As applied to freedom of speech, for example, this means that the people have such freedom simply by virtue of the fact that the Communist Party controls the press. In the words of *Red Flag,*

Is it not freedom of speech when several hundred newspapers and nearly a thousand magazines unfold contentions and debates on numerous major problems of theory and practice, such as the criterion of truth, the purpose of production, autonomy for enterprises, distribution according to labor, democracy and the legal system, the educational system, literary and artistic creation, the meaning of life, and so forth? Is it not freedom of speech when the masses of cadres and people, through letters and visits and through newspapers, magazines, television broadcasts, and other media, are criticizing the shortcomings and mistakes of party and government organizations at all levels and their workers and putting forward suggestions on work in various fields?. . .

Why is it that some people turn a blind eye to all this or write this off as not being a manifestation of freedom of speech? The problem lies in their having a totally different understanding of what is, after all, freedom of speech. Some people think that so-called freedom of speech means "speaking without any fear," speaking without any restraint, saying reactionary things without being criticized, and saying counterrevolutionary things without being punished by law. True, there is no such "freedom of speech" in our country, nor can it be allowed to exist.[77]

Citizens' Rights and State Power

If despite their lack of esteem for self-assertive individualism the writers of Chinese constitutions included rights prominently in every such document, their purpose was not to protect the individual against the state but to enable the individual to function more effectively to strengthen the state. This idea of citizens' rights as a means to a strong state was new in China, but it drew on traditional concepts to make sense.

In the late nineteenth century China was a weak monarchy invaded by strong democracies. Many Chinese considered it obvious that it was their democratic political systems that made the Western nations so strong. But at first it was difficult for minds trained in Neo-Confucianism to understand why this was so. Confucianism stressed the charisma of the emperor and his officials as the chief means of taming unruly nature and a disorderly populace. Any weakening of imperial authority was an invitation to tax evasion, banditry, natural disaster, and rebellion. But then how did Western kings and presidents not only survive the boisterous individualism of their citizens, but channel these energies to the uses of the state?

Late Qing reformers found the answer in an ancient Confucian dictum "The people are the basis of the state" (*min wei bang ben*). The line appeared in the *Book of Documents* (Shu Jing) and had been elaborated by Confucius' disciple, Mencius.[78] When Mencius was advising kings, China consisted of several weak, thinly populated states whose feuding kings were all trying to unify China and become emperor. Population was the key resource for making war. Mencius presented King Xiang of the state of Liang with a paradox: "If there were a single ruler who did not delight in slaughter, he could unite the whole world." The king asked how an unwarlike ruler could conquer his neighbors. Mencius replied, "If he were indeed such a one, the people would come to him as water flows downward, in a flood that none could hold back." Command of population would bring invincible power.

But the ruler must be skillful in husbanding this resource. When King Hui of Liang complained to Mencius that even though he gave out relief grain in bad years, people did not come to his country from neighboring kingdoms, Mencius answered that relief was not enough. The ruler must subordinate war-making to the needs of agriculture, fishery, forestry, silk-raising, animal husbandry, and moral training. Then "persons of seventy will wear silk and eat meat and the common people will suffer from neither hunger nor cold. For the ruler of such a state not to become emperor is unheard of." Rulers who squeezed their people to raise and support large armies defeated their own purposes, for the people would look on an invader as a savior. As Mencius warned King Xuan of Qi, "When . . . the inhabitants meet the invading army with flagons of drink and baskets of food, there can be only one reason: they see in the invasion a chance of escape from flood and fire."

Mencius therefore advised rulers to chose ministers who would serve the people's interests and to punish those the people disliked. In a well-ruled kingdom, he said, when the king has someone put to death, it is said that "the people killed him." Even a ruler was dispensable if he was not a good one. For example, the sage-king Wu had come to power by killing his predecessor Zhou. Mencius defended Wu from the charge of regicide on the grounds that Zhou was not a true king but a mere "robber and ruffian"—"I have heard of the cutting off of the fellow Zhou, not of the putting to death of the sovereign [Zhou]." Given that he accepted the institution of kingship, Mencius' advice to kings seemed paradoxical: "It is the people who should be valued, the gods second and the ruler last." This did not mean that the prosperity of the people was an end in itself. The point was that princes would fall if they displeased the gods and gods would be abandoned if they failed to produce good harvests, but the people could not be simply set aside. The king who would become the son of heaven had to win the people first.[79]

The late nineteenth-century reformers went back to this strand of Confucian thought, lifted it from its context and gave it a name, *minben sixiang* (the ideology of people-as-the-basis). The vogue of *minben* ideology reflected in part the rhetorical convenience of reformers appealing to a conservative and xenophobic elite. Ranging far beyond Mencius, they argued that since the classic *Guanzi* said that "the king takes the people as heaven," the king should therefore seek the approval and support of the people. Since the classic *Zuozhuan* said that "things start from a man and wife," politics should work from the bottom up. Since the *Book of Changes* said that "heaven gives birth to the people and sets up a ruler for them," the people are therefore the origin of the ruler.[80] Liang Qichao published a forced interpretation of the classics to show that ancient China had invented the idea of a parliament which had been copied by the West.[81]

But more important than rhetorical convenience was the solution which the *minben* tradition afforded to the mystery of the strength of Western democracies. Mencius' idea of the people as a resource had been further explored by later thinkers, whose thought in turn provided the basis for the reformers' interpretation. Among the most influential figures in this line of transmission were the series of Qing thinkers loosely referred to as the "statecraft school," ranging from Gu Yanwu in the early part of the Qing dynasty to Feng Guifen and others in the mid–nineteenth century. They suggested reforms in the overcentralized bureaucratic system to enable local landowners and literati to play a more active, independent role in government. They claimed that local rule would lead to greater prosperity and security and thus help strengthen the dynasty.[82] It was against the background of such ideas that the late Qing reformers forged their interpretation of democracy.

The reformers argued that Western democracies were strong because they enabled the ruler fully to use the people's energy and wisdom. In the new Darwinian world of competition among nations and races, China could no longer afford to use the people as merely a passive base for the ruler, but must mobilize them as an active source of strength. If the ruler binds and represses the people in their exercise of their natural faculties, the reformers argued, they have no way to contribute their full strength to the state. "The citizens are the substance of the state," one of the reformers argued. "The people's rights are the basis of the ruler's rights. If there are no people's rights there are no ruler's rights. . . . No ruler has ever fallen because his people were given rights."[83]

cannot be part of their legitimate purpose, and may even be damaging if it undermines the ability of the state to channel citizen energies in a unified direction.

Moreover, the *minben* tradition helps explain the preoccupation of Chinese constitution writers with providing rights for supervising, correcting, and appealing against the bureaucracy while overlooking judicial review or other channels for appeal against the rulers themselves. Of course, this concern with bureaucrats had much to do with the great size of the bureaucracy, especially after 1949, and with the long tradition of popular resentment of corrupt bureaucrats and the history of clashes between emperors and bureaucrats. As the world's oldest bureaucratic society China naturally applied its sophistication in checking and supervising bureaucrats to its modern constitutions. But the *minben* tradition also contributed to this emphasis. It made almost unthinkable an adversary relation between people and the ruler (or the ruling party) in a legitimate state. Although the relation between the citizen and the ruler could not normally be antagonistic or adversary, that between the citizen and particular bureaucrats could be. Solidarity between ruler and people was not threatened and was even enhanced by admitting that bureaucrats either blundering or corrupt might come between them. Since democracy involved rights to complain, remonstrate, appeal, and petition, it made more sense to direct these activities against particular bureaucrats than against the ruler or ruling party itself.

Finally, the *minben* tradition helps to explain the prominence of welfare rights in Chinese constitutions from the Guomindang period on. The American constitutional tradition tends to see the state's welfare obligations as second-order goals of government, to be striven for on the premise that political rights are guaranteed. In contrast, from 1931 on, Chinese constitutions placed welfare rights in a constitutional position equal to political rights. In the post-1949 constitutions, they included the rights to work, vocational training, rest, social insurance and assistance, public health facilities, retirement, education, and others.

Welfare rights are featured in the constitutions of all Marxist-Leninist states. But in Chinese political thinking their importance seems to be enhanced by the tradition of thought that sees welfare as not just one of the state's obligations to the people but its chief obligation. Of course, the *minben* tradition suggests that this obligation itself is subordinate to still higher goals — in Mencius' time uniting the empire, in modern times assuring the survival of the nation and the building of socialism. Thus in this tradition both welfare and political rights are most readily defended not as ends in themselves but as effective means to enable the citizen to contribute his energies to the state so that it can achieve its own higher purposes.[90] But welfare rights are commonly seen as the more important of the two kinds of rights, since they bear more directly on the loyalty and vigor of the people. This helps explain why Chinese policy toward political rights often limits their exercise on the grounds that excessive use could disrupt economic construction or the social order.

Political Rights and Social Utility

Political rights in modern China have most often been justified by their service to social goals, especially achieving a strong state. Both defenders and detractors of political rights subjected them to the test of social utility. In articulating this test, Chinese thinkers showed familiarity with the language of Western utilitarianism. For example, the vice chairman of the 1982 constitutional revision commission stated that "this draft is permeated by one basic principle: to serve the greatest interests of the greatest majority of the people."[91] Utilitarianism was a widely used style of argument in China throughout the twentieth century, often with explicit or implicit reference to the British Benthamite school. But the substance of Chinese views diverged greatly from that school's, drawn by the weight of many of the traditional concepts and contemporary concerns discussed so far.

Jeremy Bentham's purpose in founding the modern school of utilitarianism was to provide a basis for reform of the chaotic English legal system. His standard for good law was the greatest happiness of the greatest number, calculated by summing up the pleasure and the pain produced by an act or event for each individual affected. Bentham rejected the idea of natural rights as "nonsense upon stilts"[92] because it was part of the fabric of traditional customs and precedents he was trying to sweep away. But his philosophy remained focused on the individual because he believed it was rational for governments to enact rules that would produce the most pleasure and the least pain for the greatest possible number of individuals.

Modern Chinese thinkers were attracted by utilitarianism's idea of rational, scientific legislation, which they thought would help in the task of creating a structure of modern laws for China. They easily accepted the principle that government should work to maximize the people's welfare, which bore a strong resemblance to the traditional Mencian idea of the ruler's responsibility. But they had difficulty with Bentham's assumption that community welfare was no more than the sum of individual pleasures minus the total of individual pains. As with so many other Western ideas, the first writer to introduce utilitarianism to a Chinese audience seems to have been Liang Qichao, in a 1902 article on "The Doctrine of Bentham, Master of Utilitarianism."[93] Liang translated utilitarianism as "pleasure-and-profitism" (lelizhuyi); he knew that his Confucian-trained readers would find such a concept repugnant. He argued, though, that no matter how philosophers try to talk people out of it, pleasure and profit are still desires of human nature. The point of utilitarianism, he contended, was not to encourage selfish hedonism but to help individuals see how their pleasure and profit are tied up with the welfare of the collective. For the utilitarian principle of the greatest happiness of the greatest number, implies that "the interests of the collectivity have no separate existence apart from the interests of the constituent individuals; hence, Bentham makes the argument that public and private interest are one and the same."

In this way Liang detached Bentham's utilitarianism from its native purpose as a standard by which to judge the benefit of legislation to individuals and imposed a purpose more in keeping with contemporary Chinese preoccupations. He turned utilitarianism into a potential creed to indoctrinate the people to sacrifice personal interests for higher, common interests embodied in the state. Nor was Liang's interpretation idiosyncratic. The Chinese translation of Mill's *On Liberty* that Yan Fu brought out the following year contained the same shift of emphasis. According to Benjamin Schwartz, when "grounds of social utility or of the welfare of society are put forth [by Mill], they are not infrequently transmuted by Yan Fu into the language of the interests of the state." When Mill speaks of the development of individuality as an end in itself, Yan says that the development of strong personalities will strengthen the state. When Mill says that the individual should be allowed to do what he likes unless the interests of others are affected, Yan's translation implies that too much government interference will stifle civic virtue. Schwartz summarizes, "If liberty of the individual is often treated in Mill as an end in itself, in Yan Fu it becomes a means to the advancement of 'the people's virtue and intellect,' and beyond this to the purposes of the state."[94]

The claim that rights have social utility has been used as the chief argument for their expansion by late Qing reformers, anti-Guomindang civil libertarians, and PRC advocates of cultural and political thaw. An important example of this kind of argument was an influential 1929 essay, "On Human Rights," written by Luo Longji (1896–1965), a Western-trained professor who was probably modern China's best-known rights theorist (later a prominent victim of the Antirightist Movement of 1957). Luo defined human rights as "whatever conditions are necessary to be human, [i.e.,] (1) to support life; (2) to develop individuality and cultivate personality; (3) to attain the goal of the greatest happiness of the greatest number of the group." Freedom of speech, for example, he defended as enabling people to contribute more fully to the welfare of society. As human society advanced, more and more rights became "necessary," Luo said. The original European and American conception had been rather narrow, but "now—in 1929—in China" the people were demanding thirty-five rights. These included not only such classic items as popular sovereignty, free speech, and equality before the law, but many specific demands pointedly relevant to liberalizing the authoritarian Guomindang regime: for example, that military officers should not hold concurrent civilian government positions, that government bureaucrats should either be elected or be chosen by competitive public examination, that the tax burden should be progressive, and that government finances should be public.[95]

In authoritarian settings a Liang Qichao or a Luo Longji could use the concept of social utility to argue for a growing list of rights to meet new needs of the time. It would have been more difficult to make the same case on natural rights grounds to a Chinese audience concerned about national survival, since natural rights imply a restriction on government rather than an aid to it. But the weakness of social utility arguments lay in the fact that the authorities could so easily meet the liberals on the same ground, taking over their assumptions and using them to argue that rights must be narrowed rather than expanded for the public good. Indeed, in the crisis-ridden decades after 1895 not only the authorities but increasing numbers of intellectuals were inclined to see the greatest good of the greatest number as identical with anything that would strengthen the disastrously weak state. Liang himself converted to an authoritarian position and wrote in 1905, "even if a governmental system deprives the people of much or all of their freedom, it is a good system so long as it is founded on a spirit of meeting the necessities of national defense."[96] Sun Yat-sen explained in 1924:

Europeans rebelled and fought for liberty because they had too little liberty. But we, because we have too much liberty without any unity and resisting power, because we have become a sheet of loose sand and so have been invaded by foreign imperialism . . ., must break down individual liberty and become pressed together into an unyielding body like the firm rock which is formed by the addition of cement to sand.[97]

Under the pressure of Japanese invasion and political disorder in the 1930s, the superior utility of dictatorship seemed obvious even to former liberals. As the political science scholar Ch'ien Tuan-sheng wrote in 1934, "since dictatorship is really able to advance the welfare of the majority (which is almost all the people), then one cannot, because of the suppression of the freedoms of the minority, insist on maintaining a democracy which is not the equal of dictatorship in planning benefits."[98] One of the few Chinese intellectuals to retain his faith in democracy in the 1930s, Hu Shi, was reduced to arguing for what he called "kindergarten democracy"—the exercise of a few simple democratic rights by the people which would actually strengthen the state, he said, by encouraging more public affection for government.[99]

With Marxism came a refinement in the question of whose interests were to be served—those of the proletariat and its allies. But the principle remained the same: "All political rights, including freedom of speech, must serve the ruling class and protect the economic foundation of the society."[100] As *Red Flag* pointed out, "Democracy, like centralism, dictatorship and other political forms, is a means subordinate to the economic base. The socialist economic base determines that we must uphold the socialist democratic system, and if this democratic system does not suit the economic base, it must be reformed and improved step by step."[101] The power of deciding what degree of political freedom would serve the general interest naturally lay with the authorities. When the Party adopted economic development as its goal the Xinhua news agency asserted that "in the final analysis, the result of democracy should be measured by whether it benefits or harms our modernization program."[102] When the Politburo determined that the right of free speech should be limited by the "four basic principles" of socialism, dictatorship of the proletariat, Marxism-Leninism—Mao Zedong Thought, and Communist Party leadership, Shanghai radio declared that "in discussing democracy we must take the people's interests as the boundary line and should not break the bounds to follow the path of evil."[103] As a high-ranking party official warned, "Our society is not a park [like Hyde Park], where everyone can voice his opinion and when everyone is finished no harm has been done, no flowers or trees have been injured and everyone leaves the park and goes home." [104] Ideas were to be judged by their consequences.

Whether social utility could best be served by liberal or authoritarian institutions depended on one's evaluation of the state of the people's culture. And throughout the century, what most decisively turned the idea of social utility into an argument for authoritarianism was the widespread perception that China was backward. Bentham and Mill had proposed that different liberties were suitable at different stages of development.[105] But they were writing in an era of progress, for readers who were ready to believe that expanded freedom would be put to good use. Under the conditions of this century, few of China's rulers or even its reformers have believed for long that the Chinese people were ready for democracy. The disillusioned Liang Qichao, for example, wrote in 1903 that his countrymen did not have a single one of the qualifications necessary for citizens of a republic.[106] Rural reconstructionists like Y. C. James Yen and Liang Shuming believed that problems of peasant literacy and livelihood must be solved before the masses could exercise democracy.[107] Chiang Kai-shek defended tutelary rule on the basis of China's backwardness.[108] In 1980 Deng Xiaoping echoed Sun Yat-sen: "China has always been called a sheet of loose sand. . . . [If CCP leadership is shaken,] China will retrogress into divisions and confusion and will then be unable to accomplish modernization."[109]

Throughout the late 1970s and the early 1980s the Communist Party leadership offered a theory of the "remnants of feudalism" to explain the slow development of Chinese democracy. For example, *People's Daily* declared:

We have been building socialism in a country where feudal society prevailed for more than 2,000 years and where semifeudal and semicolonial society existed for more than 100 years. . . . The feudal system of political domination and exploitation can be overthrown by violent means, but feudalistic ideology, traditions and habits cannot be solved in this manner. Their solution is more complicated and difficult and will take a long time.[110]

Chinese communist writers argue that the problem of feudal remnants does not alter the superiority of proletarian democracy to bourgeois democracy, but means that proletarian democracy can be realized only gradually:

Proletarian democracy is history's highest form of democracy, but this does not mean that it can be put into practice immediately after the victory of the revolution. . . . After thirty years of national construction our productive power is still low and our culture is still comparatively backward. So we still can only manage the state through the proletariat's advanced stratum [the Party]. This shows the incompleteness of proletarian democracy.[111]

If throughout the century rulers used the backwardness argument to justify the restriction of rights, for a majority of reformers and liberals it mandated a softening of political demands in favor of long-term cultural, educational, and social change—a virtual flight from politics to the safer, traditionally sanctioned realm of social education. The mission most twentieth-century Chinese intellectuals set for themselves was not to change politics directly but to reform culture. Given the backwardness of the people it was necessary to accept the government's authority and work from within the system for slow change, or else disorder would ensue. This reasoning helps to explain the support which an authoritarian interpretation of rights has often received from those in Chinese society who would seem most likely to benefit from a more liberal interpretation.

Conclusion

It is no longer possible to accept the myth that the Chinese have no desire for individual rights. The important place that rights occupy in all Chinese constitutions belies it. Most recently the posters and mimeographed periodicals of Democracy Wall, the flood of appeals for rehabilitation and compensation for the injustices of the Cultural Revolution, the government's program to introduce political participation in workers' congresses and local-level peoples' congresses, and the effort to codify law and regularize legal processes all show the continuing vitality of the ideas of freedom, justice, due process, and democratic participation. This study has documented the consistent desire of twentieth-century Chinese for a democratic political order. Less extensively, it has described some of the protodemocratic and protoliberal elements in the Chinese tradition: the ideas of a moral order above politics, of the ruler's duty to assure the welfare of the people, of the individual's power and responsibility to change the world for the better.[112] The more we learn about the Chinese tradition, the less we can suppose that the tendencies of premodern Chinese thought were one-sidedly authoritarian.

Yet modern Chinese political thinkers have chosen both from their tradition and from the West those ideas that served their urgently perceived needs, and have modified foreign ideas to fit familiar patterns of thought. Since the obsessive concern of Chinese politics in this century has been with the weakness of the state, and since the dominant inherited pattern of political thought has conceived the individual as part of the group, individual rights were looked to chiefly for their contribution to establishing order in a time of chaos and creating a strong state that could protect the nation and develop it. Accordingly, Chinese constitutions were written to bestow extensive rights, but to assure at the same time that these were regulated by the state to serve its purposes. The adversarial impetus behind some Western ideas of democracy— distrust of the ruler, the desire to block tyranny, the effort to restrict and confine the powers of the state—was lacking where a strong state was the end in view. The promise of democracy was seen in its ability to unite the people behind the ruler on the basis of the two parties' shared interests. To the extent that Chinese democracy sought to check powers, it was those of the bureaucrats, viewed as coming between the people and the ruler. Instead of a system of permanent conflict among divergent interests as in the West, democracy was seen in China as a system of harmonization of diverse interests on the basis of their dominant common elements.

Moreover, as in any society, what governments actually made of rights was often not what theorists envisioned. The Communist poet and editor Feng Xuefeng addressed this point in a fable he published in 1956. A snake decides to make a law that no one can interfere with another animal's privacy without due process. Then to teach the timid hare how to use this law, the

snake barges into his den and bites one of the baby hares to death.
He waits by the door for the hare to come out and follow the new
law by charging him with breaking it.

But quite a while goes by and the hare never makes an appearance.
The snake grows annoyed. He bursts into the house finally and grabs the
hare, shouting:
"Why don't you abide by the law!"
"Sir, against whom will I use this law? Who's going to enforce it?"
"Are you afraid to take action against me?"
"Just a while ago you were the murderer. Now you're the judge. Sir,
which murderer do you want me to have arrested? Which judge do you
want me to go to?"

As if to confirm the fable's point, the author was labeled a "rightist"
and expelled from the Communist Party the year after it was published. He was not rehabilitated until more than twenty years later,
three years after his death.[113]

Critics of such misuse of law have never been lacking
in modern China; some have always taken the risk of speaking up.
But their demands, with few exceptions, fell within the dominant
tradition. The common demands of critics and reformers throughout the century centered on two points: an end to arbitrary repression of individuals by the police and political cadres, and an expanded scope of free speech so that the people could contribute
more creatively to the common goal of modernization. One is
hard-pressed to find in the voluminous writings of modern dissen-
ters any argument for self-centered individualism, for natural rights
as ends in themselves, or for the right of the people to rule without
the guidance of an elite party that supposedly knows their interests
better than they do.[114] The gap between American and Chinese
democratic values thus is wide, not only at the level of official
orthodoxies, but at the deeper level of the philosophical assumptions and cultural values that are shared within each country even
by contending ideological factions. In short, although both countries value the ideas of democracy and rights, they do so in ways
that lead to very different results.

Some argue that precisely because of this difference,
Westerners have no standing to concern themselves with the issue

of human rights in China. If human rights conceptions vary so profoundly from culture to culture, then the members of one society have no basis to comment on the conception or practice of rights in another; what the Chinese do is their own business.

A number of arguments can be advanced against this view. First, the idea of cultural relativism is itself a Western notion. The Chinese, among other peoples, are culturally universalistic in their beliefs; they believe in their own conceptions of rights and democracy and criticize "bourgeois democracy" for its failings.[115] This does not mean that they welcome foreign criticism; the Chinese government rejects foreign "interference" as an infringement on its sovereignty. But in principle most Chinese accept the validity of cross-cultural dialogue on rights issues. Second, as Louis Henkin argues in this volume, there is in fact an emerging international law of human rights which sets standards for all states, and the Chinese are moving toward acceptance of this international law.[116] Third, there are common points between the Western and Chinese conceptions of rights, such as the belief in the social usefulness of free speech. Although these points are more significant in the abstract than in application to concrete cases, they do constitute a basis for dialogue and possible mutual influence. Fourth, international attention to rights issues often encourages governments to apply their own pronounced rights values more meticulously to concrete cases than they otherwise might. Indifference on the part of foreigners removes one incentive for any government to live up to its own standards. And even if the above points were lacking, do we not finally have the obligation to give voice to the values we believe in, as others have to express theirs? It would be hard to know how to begin to talk about rights at all if it were considered improper even to discuss the differences among national systems. The alternatives are to pretend that there are no differences or to be incurious, as if the subject were not one that we cared about.

China has been changing for a century, and it is changing today. Since the death of Mao the Chinese government has been trying to establish a more stable, predictable legal and political system. The Chinese intellectual tradition contains many of the building blocks of a more liberal, pluralistic theory of rights, and the new opening to the West has made many of the resources of foreign intellectual traditions available for fresh consideration. Important constituencies for liberalizing reform—students, industrial workers, academics, writers, artists, professionals, and technicians—have gained new influence during the modernization drive. And the experience of the Cultural Revolution has given every PRC citizen, especially the leaders, a new appreciation for the importance of legal and institutional arrangements to protect individuals from arbitrary persecution. But this essay suggests the burden of the past which any major change in the character of the Chinese rights system will have to overcome. Although the rights abuses that have marked China's modern history, including the Cultural Revolution, were not mandated by the Chinese constitutions and their underlying political theories, neither were they merely the result of rulers flouting the laws. Their permissive conditions included philosophical predispositions, constitutional and legal concepts, and governmental practices that had deep roots in the past and in national values. For individual political rights to gain a different kind of footing in China would require changes far beyond the legal codification and regularization of the same rights philosophy that has been dominant for nearly a century.

Notes

1. The Human Rights Idea in Contemporary China: A Comparative Perspective

1. I draw on certain of my previous writings: *The Rights of Man Today* (Boulder, Colo.: Westview, 1978); "Rights, American and Human," *Columbia Law Review* (1979), 79:405; "Rights, Here and There," *Columbia Law Review* (1981), 81:1582. Here, as there, I have distilled from the growing and varied human rights literature, adding my own gloss. In respect to China, I have been instructed by my colleagues in this project and by writings of other China scholars.

2. Since the declaration was adopted, additional rights have been suggested. Human beings form peoples who are entitled to political self-determination and control over their own natural resources. These are included as rights in the International Covenant on Civil and Political Rights and the International Covenant on Economic, Social, and Cultural Rights. Later it was urged that there should also be recognition of a right to peace and to a healthful environment, and a right to live in a society that continues to develop politically, socially, and economically, but these have not been recognized as rights in any authoritative international instruments.

3. See the *International Bill of Rights: The Covenant on Civil and Political Rights*, Louis Henkin, ed. (New York: Columbia University Press, 1981), chs. 3, 12.

4. The right of a person to own and not to be arbitrarily deprived of property is included in the Universal Declaration. It was not incorporated into either of the covenants, principally because of differences as to how the right should be expressed, reflecting largely disagreements as to property rights for aliens. But a human right to property is generally accepted, and the Communist states accepted the Universal Declaration (with its right to property) long after they voted against inclusion of the right in the covenants. See, e.g., the Helsinki Final Act, Conference on Security and Cooperation in Europe, Principle VII (1975).

5. See, e.g., Gen. Assembly Res. 32/130, December 16, 1977.

6. There are small differences in principle and in detail: for example, the international freedom from torture and from other forms of mistreatment is more explicit and perhaps more comprehensive; the American protection against double jeopardy nevertheless permits

successive trials under federal and state law for offenses involving the same act. The Covenant on Civil and Political Rights requires a state to prohibit war propaganda and incitement to racial hatred, which the United States does not and could not do since in some contexts those prohibitions would violate the freedom of speech and press. It is not clear whether abiding private discrimination and de facto segregation on account of race, or stereotypical distinctions and private discriminations on account of gender, may violate general international standards.

7. See Professor Nathan's essay, p. 116.

8. Of course, such a constitution also makes promises, creates expectations, influences official behavior. It will not long serve its purposes if it is too far removed from what it purports to describe, or if it makes promises clearly not kept.

9. Under the 1982 constitution (art. 126), "The people's courts shall, in accordance with the law, exercise judicial power independently and are not subject to interference by administrative organs, public organizations or individuals." They are not, however, independent of political authority, and it is expressly provided that the Supreme People's Court is responsible to the National People's Congress and the latter's Standing Committee, and the local people's courts to the organs that created them (art. 128). Neither the courts nor the procuratorates have authority to enforce the constitution. See note 17.

10. Article 5 of the constitution includes: "No law . . . shall contravene the Constitution," but the rights provisions in the constitution hardly seem to limit what can be done by law. And the National People's Congress and its Standing Committee, which exercise the legislative power of the state (art. 58), also have the power to amend the constitution and to supervise its enforcement (art. 62). Amendments are adopted by majority vote of more than two-thirds of all the deputies to the Congress (art. 64).

11. Equally immutable, and superior even to the constitution, are the "four basic principles" reiterated by Deng Xiaoping: adhering to the socialist road, supporting the people's democratic dictatorship, following the leadership of the Communist Party, and taking Marxism-Leninism—Mao Zedong Thought as the guiding ideology.

12. The comparable provision in the earlier published draft provided that "the rights of citizens are inseparable from their duties" (draft art. 32). The change, if it is more than a difference in translation, does not appear to have any significance.

13. In China, moreover, there is—perhaps inevitably—some confusion between the needs of socialism and the needs and interests of the socialist state, and of a particular socialist state at a particular time, as determined by particular leaders.

14. Many Chinese laws and regulations are unpublished, and applicable law is often difficult to ascertain, thus weakening the protections of legality for the individual and its restraints on the official.

15. A right to counsel is provided by the Criminal Procedure Code, articles 26–30. The significance of that right is different from what it is in the United States because of the narrow role played by defense lawyers.

16. Compare article 4 of the Covenant on Civil and Political Rights (p. 10 above) permitting derogation from most (but not all) rights only "in time of public emergency which threatens the life of the nation" and only "to the extent strictly required by the exigencies of the situation."

17. The 1978 constitution provided that "citizens have the right to appeal to organs of state at any level against any infringement of their rights" (art. 55). And the Supreme People's Procuratorate was to exercise "procuratorial authority to ensure observance of the Constitution and the law by all the departments under the State Council, the local organs of state

at various levels, the personnel of organs of state and the citizens" (art. 43). The 1982 constitution provides that "citizens have the right to make to relevant state organs complaints and charges against, or exposures of, any state organ or functionary, for violation of the law or dereliction of duty" (art. 41). The procuratorates, including the Supreme People's Procuratorate, are "state organs for legal supervision" (art. 129), but there is no mention of any responsibility or power to ensure observance of the constitution. Compare note 9.

2. Civil and Social Rights: Theory and Practice in Chinese Law Today

1. For general discussion, see Richard Bernstein, *From the Center of the Earth* (Boston: Little, Brown, 1982); and Fox Butterfield, *China: Alive in the Bitter Sea* (New York: Times Books, 1982).

2. See for example an article by Liu Han and Wu Daying, "Shenme shi 'renquan'? Woguo xianfa he falü weishenme buyong 'renquan' yici?" *Minzhu yu fazhi* (September 1979) 2:21. They state:

Our constitution employs the scientific concept of citizens' basic rights which not only includes the rational content of the term 'human rights' but also revolutionizes the term. . . . Hence, the exclusion of the term human rights from our constitution does not indicate our objection to human rights. . . . The slogan of protecting human rights represents the opposition to maltreatment, torture, discrimination, persecution and other forms of brutal insult to the person and his character. . . . The proletariat does not negate human rights. As for a very small number of scum in our society who, completely lacking patriotism and disregarding national dignity and personal integrity, have subserviently requested foreigners to "be concerned" about the problem of "human rights" in China, it is a different matter. The criticism of this tiny minority by the masses of the people is absolutely necessary.

3. For the Chinese language texts of constitutional documents promulgated in Communist-held areas betweeen 1930 and 1948, see Han Yanlong and Chang Zhaoru, eds., *Zhongguo xin minzhuzhuyi geming shiqi genjudi fazhi wenxian xuanbian*, 3 vols. (Beijing: Zhongguo shehui kexue chubanshe, 1981) (hereafter cited as *Selected Legal Documents*), 1:1–109. For a somewhat unreliable English translation of one of the earliest of these documents, the seventeen-article Constitutional Program of the Jiangxi Soviet Republic, see W. E. Butler, trans. and ed., *Legislation of the Chinese Soviet Republic (1931–1934)* (London: University College Monograph Series 2, 1981), pp. 1–6.

4. Leo Goodstadt, "China's New Constitution: Maoism, Economic Change, and Civil Liberties," *Hong Kong Law Journal* (September 1978), 8(3):291.

5. *Ibid.*, p. 292.

6. J. A. Cohen, "China's Changing Constitution," *China Quarterly* (December 1978), 76:836–837.

7. *Ibid.*, p. 840.

8. The "four great freedoms" refer to the rights spawned by the Cultural Revolution to "speak out freely, air their views fully, hold great debates, and write big-character posters" (art. 45 of the 1978 constitution).

9. For a report on differences of opinion among people's deputies over the issue of elimination of the right to post big-character posters, see "Controversy Over Big-Character Posters," *Beijing Review* (1979) 22(28):21–22.

10. Wang Shuwen, "Lun xianfa de zui gao falü xiaoli," *Faxue yanjiu* (1981), 1:2–3.

11. Yu Haocheng, "Yige jiqi zhongyao de jianyi: guanyu xianfa shishi de baozhang wenti," *Faxue zazhi* (1982), 4:23–27.

12. Interviews with former residents of China conducted in Hong Kong and New York in the mid- to late 1970s reflected widespread skepticism about the significance of constitutional rights provisions. Confirmation of past disregard for constitutional provisions regarding citizens' rights is offered by Feng Wenbin, Vice President of the CCP Party School, in an article entitled "Reforming the Political Structure," *Beijing Review* (1981), 24(4):17–20, 28; Feng declares: "In the past our cadres did not have a strong concept of rule by law. . . . Even the Constitution and laws in general became mere scraps of paper and there was no safeguard for the people's rights."

13. Commentator, "Lue tan renquan wenti," *Guangming ribao* on October 26, 1979, excerpted in *Beijing Review* (1979), 22(45):17–20.

14. Sheng Zuhong, "Renquan yu fazhi," *Minzhu yu fazhi* (September 1979), 2:19–20.

15. For example, see Shen Baoxiang, Wang Chengquan, and Li Zerui, "On the Question of Human Rights in the International Realm," *Beijing Review* (1982), 25(30):13–17, 22; and see Yu Xiao, "Guoji fa renquan wenti jianjie," *Faxue zazhi* (1980), 3:54–56.

16. See particularly Wang Tieya, chief ed., *Guoji fa* (Beijing: Falü chubanshe, 1981), p. 99. Wang's book is a standard law textbook.

17. *Selected Works of Mao Zedong* (Peking: Foreign Languages Press, 1961–1977), 5:299–300.

18. Peng Zhen, "Guanyu Zhonghua renmin gongheguo xianfa xiugai caoan de baogao," *Fazhi bao*, December 10, 1982, p. 1. Also see *Beijing Review* (1982), 25(50):13.

19. For a discussion of the reasons for the PRC government's ban on rural migration to the cities, see William Parish, "Socialism and the Chinese Peasant Family," *Journal of Asian Studies* (May 1975), 34(3):625–626.

20. "Lun woguo gongmin de jiben quanli he yiwu," *Faxue zazhi* (1982), 24(4):20.

21. *Renmin ribao*, July 31, 1980, p. 5.

22. *Selected Legal Documents*, 1:60.

23. See generally "China's Procuratorates," *Beijing Review* (1979), 22(52):16–19.

24. For example, see "Equality Before the Law," in *Beijing Review* (1981), 24(41):26–27, excerpting an article from *People's Daily* of August 31, 1981. After reporting the division of China's legal profession over the proper definition of "equality before the law," the author chooses the more narrow definition, declaring, "If we say that 'everybody is equal' in the legislative process at the present stage, it would mean to negate the class nature of law."

25. See letter to the editor of *Minzhu yu fazhi* (1979), 3:30, complaining that while the newspapers are loudly proclaiming the principle of "equality before the law," in real life the phenomenon of inequality is quite common. The author cites as an example a case where two Huangpu policemen beat up a citizen and were given only the rather mild sanction of a "warning"; the letter implies that the citizen would be subjected to a far more severe punishment if he were to beat a policeman.

26. Thus, while invoking the popular and ancient Chinese metaphor of "100 flowers blooming and 100 schools of thought contending" (originally conceived to describe a situation of complete freedom and great variety of creative thought and expression), Chen Pixian told an assembly of law professors:

Upholding the Four Basic Principles is the most important political criterion in editing teaching materials. . . . We advocate the "simultaneous blooming of one hundred flowers and the contention of one hundred schools of thought," but the "blooming and contending" to which we refer must be carried out under the guidance of Marxism-Leninism and Mao Zedong Thought.

"Zai faxue jiaocai zuotanhuishang de jianghua" (December 3, 1982), *Fazhi bao*, December 24, 1982, p. 1. For an exposition of the point that upholding the "four basic principles" is the guiding tenet of the new constitution, see "Xin xianfa de zong de zhidao sixiang" by Wang Shuwen, Director of the Institute of Law, in the same issue of *Fazhi bao*, p. 3. See also the speech by Peng Zhen at the founding meeting of the China Law Association on July 22, 1982, where he criticizes legal researchers who are influenced by the ideas of Greece, Rome, and the European Renaissance and Enlightenment, or indeed by any abstract theory. Stating that there is only one objective reality, Peng urges realism as a means of achieving the goal of unity of thought in legal circles. "Fazhan shehuizhuyi minzhu, jian-quan shehuizhuyi fazhi," in *Fazhi bao*, October 1, 1982, p. 1.

27. *Selected Legal Documents*, 1:66–71. See art. 7, p. 68, and art. 6, p. 69.

28. *Ibid.*, p. 11; see art. 13.

29. See T. Gelatt, "The Bounds of Free Expression," *Asian Wall Street Journal*, December 18, 1979. Also see an editorial in *China Daily*, August 4, 1982, entitled "How to Ascertain Whether Speech is a Criminal Act."

30. For a remarkable essay on the dangers of punishing speech, see "On Freedom of Speech," by Hu Ping, in *SPEAHRhead* (Winter/Spring 1982), 12/13:35–50. Hu Ping was elected Peking University's delegate to the local people's congress. The CCP Central Committee issued a directive forbidding republication of Hu's writings; it did not block his election, but he was not permitted to take his seat.

31. *Renmin ribao*, December 14, 1980, p. 3.

32. See the report of the speech by Deng Xiaoping asserting that this freedom to post big-character posters had been abused by "ultra-individualists like Wei Jingsheng," and announcing that the freedom would be excised from the constitution at the next session of the NPC. *New York Times*, January 18, 1980, p. A2.

33. See James Seymour, ed., *The Fifth Modernization: China's Human Rights Movement, 1978–1979* (Stanfordville, N.Y.: Human Rights Publishing Group, 1980), a collection of primary documents from the "Peking Spring" democracy movement. This episode and the dissident demand for greater democracy and human rights protection are also treated in Fox Butterfield's *China*, and Richard Bernstein's *From the Center*.

34. See "Freedom of Divorced Affirmed," in *Beijing Review* (1980), 23(43):8. Compare Butterfield, *China*, pp. 173–176.

35. Enacted in June 1979, both codes went into effect on January 1, 1980. For Chinese texts see *Diwujie quanguo renmin daibiao dahui de erci huiyi wenjian* (Beijing: Renmin chubanshe, 1979).

36. For example, see Peng Zhen, Director of the Commission for Legal Affairs of the NPC, "Explanation on Seven Laws"; Peng declares: "During the Cultural Revolution, the widespread practice of extortion of confessions through torture, the 'beating, smashing, and looting,' and the unlawful incarceration and persecution on false charges perpetrated by Lin Biao and the Gang of Four led to extremely grave consequences with numerous cases of people being unjustly, falsely and wrongly charged and sentenced." *Beijing Review* (1979), 22(28):11. Also see interview with Sha Qiuli, noted jurist and deputy director of the NPC Legal Affairs Commission; Sha says: "Our Constitution has explicitly stated the fundamental rights of the citizen. Previously, however, such rights were not guaranteed. Infringement of citizens' rights constantly occurred. Especially. . . under Lin Biao and the

Gang of Four, innocent people were framed at random." NCNA, Beijing, July 6, 1979, in FBIS, July 6, 1979, p. L14. Also note the call issued by Jiang Hua, President of the Supreme People's Court, for elimination of illegal practices "that insult the human dignity and violate the individual personal rights of the criminal, such as struggling in rotation, parading before the masses, and repeated sentencing in public," in "Duanzheng sixiang luxian, yingjie xin de changzheng," *Minzhu yu fazhi* (1979), 2:4.

   37. Christopher S. Wren, "China Moves to Resurrect a Credible Legal System," *New York Times,* December 5, 1982, pp. A1, A22.

   38. *Guowuyuan gongbao,* August 20, 1981, 12:368.

   39. Wren, "China Moves," pp. A1, A22.

   40. For example, see Christopher S. Wren, "Crime and Capital Punishment in China," *New York Times,* November 20, 1983, p. E9.

   41. See an article in favor of the presumption of innocence, in *Minzhu yu fazhi* (1979), 4:15; and a rebuttal in the same journal (1980), 3:20–21.

   42. See Zhou Zheng, "Visits and Letters from the People," *Beijing Review* (1982), 25(25):23–28; this system, established in the early 1950s, "helps inform the Party and government of the people's demands and strengthens the people's supervision over cadres" (p. 23). The article notes that in the city of Shashi the city government and the Party committee share an office that in 1981 received 957 letters and 1,268 visits (p. 26). For further information on the nature and importance of "letters and visits" in redressing miscarriages of justice, see "Zhengque duidai shangfang wenti," *Renmin ribao,* October 22, 1979, p. 1. Other reports on this practice are contained in *Renmin ribao* on September 9, 1979, p. 1; October 5, 1979, p. 1; October 21, 1979, p. 1; October 28, 1979, p. 1; and November 10, 1979, p. 4.

   43. This sanction was established by statute enacted on August 3, 1957. *Zhonghua renmin gongheguo fagui huibian,* Guowuyuan fazhiju, comp. (Beijing: Falü chubanshe, 1958), 6:243–244. See discussion in Jerome Alan Cohen, *The Criminal Process in the People's Republic of China, 1949–1963: An Introduction* (Cambridge: Harvard University Press, 1968), p. 249 ff. The statute was revised slightly in 1979 to provide for a joint committee to approve application of the sanction. The committee is made up of representatives of the police, the urban civil affairs bureau, and the labor bureau. See "Supplementary Regulations," FBIS, November 30, 1979, p. L3. The revised regulations stipulate that offenders who have completed "labor education" are not to be discriminated against in subsequent job assignments or admission to educational institutions. See also discussion of this sanction by Wren, "China Moves," p. A22.

   44. Thus, in the "commentator's" article on "Notes on the Human Rights Question" (*supra* note 13), it is stated that "only by raising economic and cultural levels can citizen rights of democracy and freedom be fully realized."

   45. Thus, article 42, which provides that citizens have the right and obligation to work, explicitly links the improvement of labor conditions to increased production. Improved satisfaction of the rights to rest and to receive social welfare is also implicitly conditioned on improved economic circumstances (arts. 43 and 45). This point is made forcefully by the *Guangming ribao* editorial cited in note 13, *supra:* "Any right is invariably restricted by certain material conditions and cultural levels. Without a relatively developed economy, it will be difficult to enable every citizen to enjoy fully the right to work and rest and other economic rights." Commenting on the 1982 draft constitution, and praising its realistic quality, Wu Jialin states in "Lun woguo gongmin de jiben quanli he yiwu," "The basic rights and duties of citizens, particularly economic and cultural rights, must be subject to

the constraints of the level of development of the productive forces." In *Faxue zazhi* (1982), 4:20.

46. *Selected Legal Documents*, 1:9–10.

47. *Fazhi bao*, September 26, 1980, p. 3.

48. Xiao Weiyun, "Weishenme yao xiugai xianfa?" *Fazhi bao*, May 21, 1982, p. 3.

49. *Renmin ribao*, June 2, 1982, p. 4.

50. For an article describing how a factory in Guangdong Province implemented the new national policy calling for shifting factory decision-making power from the Party committee to the worker's congress, see *People's Daily*, November 20, 1980, p. 2.

51. See Wu Jialin, "Commentary," *supra* note 45, p. 20. Also see Christopher Wren, "China To Get New Constitution Tomorrow, Its 4th Since 1949," *New York Times*, December 3, 1982, p. A14. Wren quotes a delegate to the NPC as saying, "In China, where enterprises and their products are owned by the people themselves, to strike would impair the interests of the people, including the workers."

52. Article 5 of the Chinese Soviet Constitution of 1931, in *Selected Legal Documents*, 1:9–10.

53. See Parish, "Socialism and the Chinese Peasant Family," p. 616.

54. *Selected Legal Documents*, 1:11.

55. *Selected Legal Documents*, 1:60.

56. Butterfield, *China*, p. 197.

57. For example, see Yu Xiao, "Guoji fa renquan wenti jianjie," *Faxue zazhi* (1980), 3:55.

3. Political Rights in Chinese Constitutions

1. Henry Shue, *Basic Rights: Subsistence, Affluence, and U.S. Foreign Policy* (Princeton: Princeton University Press, 1980).

2. Louis Henkin, *The Rights of Man Today* (Boulder: Westview Press, 1978), p. 31.

3. See, e.g., Zhou Xiaming, "On Freedom," *Red Flag*, no. 8 (April 16, 1981), in Joint Publications Research Service (hereafter JPRS), 78358:58; *Beijing Review* (1982), 25(30):17.

4. Twelve pre-1949 constitutions and major drafts are listed in Ch'ien Tuan-sheng, *The Government and Politics of China, 1912–1949*, paperback ed. (Stanford: Stanford University Press, 1970), p. 435. Since that time the PRC has promulgated four constitutions. The eleven texts I have selected are listed in table 1.

5. S. E. Finer, ed., *Five Constitutions* (Atlantic Highlands, N.J.: Humanities Press, 1979), p. 82 (Britain), p. 27 (France).

6. See, e.g., Louis Henkin, "Constitutional Fathers—Constitutional Sons," *Minnesota Law Review* (June 1976), 60(6):1113–1147.

7. Except as otherwise noted, the text of this and other constitutional documents discussed below can be found in Zhang Jinfan and Zeng Xianyi, *Zhongguo xianfa shilüe* (Beijing: Beijing chubanshe, 1979), appendix 2. Translations are mine throughout. English translations of *Principles of the Constitution* may be found in Norbert Meienberger, *The Emergence of Constitutional Government in China (1905–1908)* (Bern: Peter Lang, 1980), pp. 91–93, and in Pao Chao Hsieh, *The Government of China (1644–1911)*, reprint ed. (New York: Octagon Books, 1978), pp. 371–373.

8. Cited in Maribeth E. Cameron, *The Reform Movement in China, 1898–1912*, reprint ed. (New York: Octagon Books, 1963), p. 103.

9. Quoted in Zhang and Zeng, *Zhongguo xianfa*, p. 70 (see n. 7).

10. Ge Gongzhen, *Zhongguo baoxue shi*, reprint ed. (Taibei: Xuesheng shuju, 1964), p. 424. The Printed Matter Statute of the same year required publications to register and submit copies of their publications; Ge, *Baoxue*, pp. 416–424.

11. The texts may be found in Yang Youjiong, *Jindai Zhongguo lifa shi*, expanded ed. (Taibei: Shangwu yinshuguan, 1966), pp. 53–55; English translations in Meienberger, *Emergence of Constitutional Government*, pp. 93–94, and Hsieh, *Government of China*, pp. 373–374.

12. P'eng-yüan Chang, "The Constitutionalists," in Mary Clabaugh Wright, ed., *China in Revolution: The First Phase, 1900–1913*, paperback ed., pp. 143–183 (New Haven: Yale University Press, 1968), and "Political Participation and Political Elites in Early Republican China: The Parliament of 1913–1914," Andrew J. Nathan, tr., *Journal of Asian Studies* (February 1978), 37(2):293–296; Cameron, *Reform Movement*, pp. 120–133. Only 98 provincial delegates were actually chosen.

13. Lee-hsia Hsu Ting, *Government Control of the Press in Modern China, 1900–1949* (Cambridge: East Asian Research Center, Harvard University, 1974), pp. 12–13. Although this law was published while Yuan's Constitutional Compact was in effect, it continued in force after the Provisional Constitution was restored.

14. Chang, "Political Participation and Political Elites," pp. 294–297.

15. Andrew J. Nathan, *Peking Politics, 1918–1923: Factionalism and the Failure of Constitutionalism* (Berkeley: University of California Press, 1976).

16. Ch'ien, *Government and Politics*, pp. 133–137; Yang, *Jindai Zhongguo lifa*, p. 354 (see n. 11).

17. "Zhongguo Guomindang diyici quanguo daibiao dahui xuanyan," in *Geming wenxian*, 8:123–124. For a commentary on the meaning of this passage, see Chen Zhimai, *Zhongguo zhengfu* (Shanghai: Shangwu yinshuguan, 1945), p. 26.

18. Sa Mengwu, quoted in Lloyd E. Eastman, *The Abortive Revolution: China Under Nationalist Rule, 1927–1937* (Cambridge: Harvard University Press, 1974), p. 150.

19. "Queding xunzheng shiqi dang zhengfu renmin xingshi zhengquan zhiquan zhi fenji ji fanglüe an," *Geming wenxian*, 23:432–433. Also see "Shi zuzhi fa" (1930), articles 6 and 7, in *Cengding Guomin zhengfu sifa ligui*, Sifa yuan canshi chu, comp. (Nanjing, 1931), 1:261–262; "Guomin dahui daibiao xuanju fa" (1936), articles 3 and 12, in *Gaiding Guomin zhengfu sifa ligui*, Sifa yuan canshi chu, comp. (Nanjing, 1936), 2:3991–3992.

20. Eastman, *Abortive Revolution*, pp. 25–30; Ch'ien, *Government and Politics*, pp. 311–312; W. Y. Tsao, *The Constitutional Structure of Modern China* (Carlton, Victoria: Melbourne University Press, 1947), pp. 61–66; *The Chinese Year Book, 1937 Issue*, compiled by Council of International Affairs (Shanghai: Commercial Press, 1937), pp. 1093, 1113.

21. Ch'ien, *Government and Politics*, p. 134.

22. Ch'ien, *Government and Politics*, pp. 191–204; quotation from p. 192.

23. Ch'ien, *Government and Politics*, p. 139; on the National Assembly, pp. 313–324; on the People's Political Council, pp. 278–285; on the Organic Law of National Government, p. 151.

24. Eastman, *Abortive Revolution*, pp. 20–30, 74–77.

25. Hu Shi, "Renquan yu yuefa," in Liang Shiqiu, Hu Shi, and Luo Longji, *Renquan lunji* (Shanghai: Xinyue shudian, 1930), p. 8.

26. An English translation is in Ch'ien, *Government and Politics*, appendix D.

27. Tao Baichuan, comp., *Zuixin liufa quanshu* (Taibei: Sanmin shuju gufen youxian gongsi, 1980), pp. 18–19.

28. Tsao, *Constitutional Structure*, p. 58.

29. Ming-min Peng, "Political Offenses in Taiwan: Laws and Problems," *China Quarterly* (July/September 1971), 47:471–493; "Taiwan (Republic of China)," Amnesty International Briefing Paper no. 6, second ed. (London: Amnesty International, 1980).

30. For example, "Defense Minister Discusses Martial Law," *Chung-yang jih-pao*, September 22, 1982, in Foreign Broadcast Information Service, *Daily Report: China* (hereafter FBIS), September 28, 1982, p. V1.

31. Ch'ien, *Government and Politics*, p. 331–345; Hungdah Chiu and Jyh-pin Fa, "Law and Justice Since 1966," in James C. Hsiung et al., eds., *Contemporary Republic of China: The Taiwan Experience, 1950–1980*, paperback ed., pp. 315–316 (New York: American Association for Chinese Studies, 1981).

32. Jyh-pin Fa, *A Comparative Study of Judicial Review Under Nationalist Chinese and American Constitutional Law*, Occasional Papers/Reprints Series in Contemporary Asian Studies, no. 4–1980 (33), School of Law, University of Maryland, pp. 97 157.

33. The discussion which follows is based on the 1934 text found in Zhang and Zeng, *Zhongguo xianfa* (see n. 7), pp. 355–358. A translation of questionable reliability exists; see Professor Edwards' essay, note 3. For an English translation of the 1931 version, see Conrad Brandt, Benjamin Schwartz, and John K. Fairbank, *A Documentary History of Chinese Communism*, paperback ed. (New York: Atheneum, 1966), pp. 220–224.

34. Articles 5 and 7. Chinese text in Chen Hefu, ed., *Zhongguo xianfa leibian* (Beijing: Zhongguo shehui kexue chubanshe, 1980), pp. 183–194; English text in Theodore H. E. Chen, ed., *The Chinese Communist Regime: Documents and Commentary* (New York: Praeger, 1967), pp. 34–45.

35. Zhang and Zeng, *Zhongguo xianfa*, p. 243.

36. Dong Chengmei, "Nationals, Citizens, and People," *Guangming ribao*, February 2, 1980, p. 3, in FBIS, February 14, 1980, p. L9.

37. Li Buyun and Zhou Yuanqing, "Falü yu ziyou," *Hongqi* (November 16, 1981), 22:17. Also see Zhang Xin, "Zhongguo shehuizhuyi xianfa gainian yu shijian," part 1, *Mingbao yuekan* (December 1983), 18(12):22.

38. Zhang and Zeng, *Zhongguo xianfa*, p. 359 (see note 7).

39. James Pinckney Harrison, *The Long March to Power: A History of the Chinese Communist Party, 1921–1972* (New York: Praeger, 1972), pp. 204, 235.

40. This structure was summarized in the Shaan-Gan-Ning Border Region Constitutional Principles of 1946; the text is in Zhang and Zeng, *Zhongguo xianfa*, pp. 358–360 (see n. 7). On the history of the councils see Mark Selden, *The Yenan Way in Revolutionary China* (Cambridge: Harvard University Press, 1971), pp. 121–176; and James R. Townsend, *Political Participation in Communist China*, new edition (Berkeley: University of California Press, 1969), pp. 58–63.

41. Karl Marx, "The Civil War in France," in Robert C. Tucker, ed., *The Marx-Engels Reader*, second ed., p. 632 (New York: Norton, 1978).

42. Selden, *Yenan Way*, pp. 121–176, and Harrison, *Long March*, pp. 204–209, 313–318.

43. Brandt, Schwartz, and Fairbank, *Documentary History*, p. 423. Also see Townsend, *Political Participation*, p. 46.

44. Mao is quoted by John Bryan Starr, *Continuing the Revolution: The Political Thought of Mao* (Princeton: Princeton University Press, 1979), p. 196.

45. An English translation is in Chen, ed., *Chinese Communist Regime*, pp. 75–92.

46. *Selected Works of Mao Tsetung* (Peking: Foreign Languages Press, 1961–1977), 5:146.

47. Li Da, *Zhonghua renmin gongheguo xianfa jianghua* (Beijing: Renmin chubanshe, 1956), p. 206.

48. Mao, *Selected Works*, 5:144.

49. Li Da, *Jianghua*, pp. 206, 210.

50. FBIS, April 14, 1980, pp. L7–L11.

51. G. Raymond Nunn, *Publishing in Mainland China*, M.I.T. report no. 4 (Cambridge: M.I.T. Press, 1966), appendix A.

52. Jerome Alan Cohen, *The Criminal Process in the People's Republic of China, 1949– 1963: An Introduction* (Cambridge: Harvard University Press, 1968), pp. 299–302.

53. *Ibid.*, p. 215.

54. *Ibid.*, p. 249.

55. This and much of the following information, unless otherwise noted, comes from Zhang Lingjie, "Tan boxue zhengzhi quanli," *Faxue yanjiu* (December 23, 1981), 6:6– 10. For the relevant laws in the Jiangxi and Shaan-Gan-Ning periods, see Patricia E. Griffin, *The Chinese Communist Treatment of Counterrevolutionaries: 1924–1949* (Princeton: Princeton University Press, 1976), appendices. For further relevant information see Cohen, *Criminal Process*, pp. 277–278, 308–309, 519–522. On the class system in general, see Richard Curt Kraus, *Class Conflict in Chinese Socialism* (New York: Columbia University Press, 1981). A few items of information in the following discussion come from interviews with émigrés and legal specialists from China.

56. See, for example, Beijing Xinhua, report of August 28, 1980, in FBIS, August 28, 1980, p. L15.

57. Han Mingli and Guo Yuzhao, "Democracy Is a State System—Also Discussing Its Relationship with Legality," *Faxue yanjiu*, no. 3 (June 23, 1980), in JPRS, 76466: 60.

58. Hu quoted in FBIS, June 23, 1980, p. L1; twenty million figure from *Renmin ribao*, November 2, 1984, p. 4; also see Gordon A. Bennett, "Political Labels and Popular Tension," *Current Scene* (February 26, 1969), 7(4):20. Richard L. Walker has estimated that between thirty-two million and sixty million persons died in various political campaigns and in the course of undergoing labor reform from 1949 to about 1971. Most of these persons would have been deprived of political rights as part of their punishment. See Richard L. Walker, "The Human Cost of Communism in China," printed for the use of the Committee on the Judiciary, U.S. Senate (Washington, D.C.: Government Printing Office, 1971), p. 16.

59. Zhang, "Tan boxue," p. 9.

60. As provided in the 1953 Electoral Law; the text is in Chen, *Chinese Communist Regime*, pp. 65–75.

61. See the 1956 Communist Party constitution in Chen, *Chinese Communist Regime*, pp. 127–148, especially the section on "General Program" and article 59.

62. Feng Wenbin, "On the Question of Socialist Democracy," second installment, *Renmin ribao*, November 25, 1980, p. 5, in FBIS, December 2, 1980, p. L9. Wang Shuwen and Zhou Yanrui, "New Development of the People's Congress System," *Faxue yanjiu*, no. 3 (1982), in JPRS, 81777:25. For meeting dates of the NPC, see John L. Scherer, ed., *China Facts and Figures Annual* (Gulf Breeze, Fla.: Academic International Press, 1978), 1:19–20. On local congresses and elections see Townsend, *Political Participation*, pp. 103–137.

63. See "Organic Law of the People's Procuratorates" of 1954 in Chen, *Chinese Communist Regime*, pp. 99–104.

64. Jerome Alan Cohen, "China's Changing Constitution," *China Quarterly* (December 1978), 76:802.

65. Chinese texts of these constitutions may be found in Chen, ed., *Zhongguo xianfa* (see n. 34), pp. 1–18 and 333–343, and in *Renmin ribao*, December 5, 1982, pp. 1–3. English texts may be found in *Peking Review* (1975), 18(4):12–17; (1978), 21(11):5–14; and *Beijing Review* (1982), 25(52):10–29.

66. Mao, *Selected Works*, 5:345. One of the earliest, if not the earliest, mentions of the right to strike in a Chinese Communist constitutional document occurred in the "Draft Program for a Basic State Law (Constitution) for the Chinese Soviet Republic" of 1930, but the right was dropped when the Jiangxi Program was adopted the following year. For the text of the Draft Program see Han Yanlong and Chang Zhaoru, eds., *Zhongguo xin min-zhuzhuyi geming shiqi genjudi fazhi wenxian xuanbian*, 3 vols. (Beijing: Zhongguo shehui kexue chubanshe, 1981), 1:3–7.

67. Fox Butterfield, *China: Alive in the Bitter Sea* (New York: Times Books, 1982), p. 324.

68. *Peking Review* (1975), 18(4):19.

69. Townsend, *Political Participation*, pp. 122–123; *Renmin ribao*, January 1, 1979, p. 6; Contributing Reporter, "Some Current Problems in Drafting Laws," *Guangming ribao*, December 22, 1978, p. 3, in FBIS, January 4, 1979, pp. E7–E10.

70. Yeh Chien-ying, "Report on the Revision of the Constitution," *Peking Review* (1978), 21(11):22.

71. *Beijing Review* (1980), 23(40):22.

72. *Beijing Review* (1980), 23(11):17.

73. *Beijing Review* (1981), 24(36):16–19.

74. See, e.g., *Beijing Review* (1982), 25(25):23–28.

75. "Organic Law of the Local People's Congresses and Local People's Governments of the People's Republic of China," FBIS, July 27, 1979, supplement 019, pp. 1–12; "Electoral Law of the PRC for the NPC and Local People's Congresses at All Levels," *ibid.*, pp. 12–19. The NPC passed appropriate amendments to make the constitution consistent with these laws; *Beijing Review* (1979), 22(28):10.

76. Andrew J. Nathan, *Chinese Democracy* (New York: Knopf, 1985), ch. 10.

77. See coverage in *Renmin ribao* at the time of the session.

78. "The Organic Law of the People's Procuratorates of the People's Republic of China," FBIS, July 27, 1979, supplement 019, pp. 27–33.

79. *Beijing Review* (1982), 23(19):18.

80. *Beijing Review* (1982), 25(19):20.

81. Interview; for guarded published references to this issue, see Xie Cichang and Xu Dengqing, "Dangqian guonei faxue de yixie dongxiang," *Renmin ribao*, January 27, 1981, p. 5; Pan Nianzhi and Qi Naikuan, "On 'Everyone Is Equal Before the Law,' " *Guangming ribao*, February 9, 1980, p. 3, in FBIS, February 25, 1980, pp. L14–L15.

82. *Beijing Review* (1982), 25(19):20.

83. *Beijing Review* (1982), 25(50):13.

84. For example, Yu Haocheng, "The New Constitution Has Developed Socialist Democracy," *Renmin ribao*, December 20, 1982, in FBIS, December 28, 1982, p. K14.

85. Dong Likun, "No One Can Stand Above the Law: A Discussion of the Relationships Between the Law and Individuals, the Party, the Government and Policies," *Shehui kexue*, no. 1 (February 1980), in JPRS, 77155:15; Pan Nianzhi, "Some Ideas About Revising the Constitution," *Minzhu yu fazhi*, no. 4 (April 20, 1981), in JPRS, 78450:35.

86. The term "four basic principles" was not mentioned, but each of the principles was. Official commentary stressed their mandatory character. See, e.g., Lin Liangqi, "The Four Basic Principles Represent the Fundamental Guiding Ideology in Revising the Constitution," *Hongqi*, no. 10 (May 16, 1982), in FBIS, May 28, 1982, pp. K6–K9; editorial, "Adhering to the Four Basic Principles Is the General Guiding Thought for Revising the Constitution," *Renmin ribao*, May 24, 1982, in FBIS, May 25, 1982, pp. K1–K3.

87. E.g., Cheng Jiyong, "The Constitution Should Effectively Guarantee the Democratic Rights of Citizens," *Shehui kexue*, no. 3 (1981), translated in JPRS, 79239:4.

88. "Zhonghua renmin gongheguo minzu quyu zizhifa," *Renmin ribao*, June 4, 1984, pp. 1–2.

89. See, e.g., Wu Jialing, "How to Bring Into Play the Function of the National People's Congress as the Organ of Supreme State Power," *Guangming ribao*, October 30, 1980, in FBIS, November 25, 1980, pp. L29–L33.

90. For a point by point comparison of the Principles and the Meiji Constitution see Hsieh, *Government of China*, p. 353.

91. See, for example, Henkin, "Constitutional Fathers"; Ronald Dworkin, *Taking Rights Seriously*, paperback ed. (Cambridge: Harvard University Press, 1978).

4. Sources of Chinese Rights Thinking

A shorter version of this chapter appears as chapter 6 in Andrew J. Nathan, *Chinese Democracy* (New York: Knopf, 1985).

1. Louis Henkin, *The Rights of Man Today* (Boulder: Westview Press, 1978), p. 7.

2. Derk Bodde and Clarence Morris, *Law in Imperial China Exemplified by 190 Ch'ing Dynasty Cases* (Cambridge: Harvard University Press, 1967), pp. 1–51.

3. Wm. Theodore deBary, "Chinese Despotism and the Confucian Ideal: A Seventeenth-Century View," in John K. Fairbank, ed., *Chinese Thought and Institutions*, paperback ed., p. 195 (Chicago: University of Chicago Press, 1967). Reference is specifically to the thought of Huang Zongxi.

4. On Liang Qichao in general, see Hao Chang, *Liang Ch'i-ch'ao and Intellectual Transition in China, 1890–1907* (Cambridge: Harvard University Press, 1971) and Philip C. Huang, *Liang Ch'i-ch'ao and Modern Chinese Liberalism* (Seattle: University of Washington Press, 1972). Liang's essays on Hobbes and Rousseau are in *Yinbing shi wenji* (hereafter abbreviated YBSWJ), reprint ed. (Taibei: Zhonghua shuju, 1960), vol. 3, *juan* 6, pp. 89–94 and 97–110.

5. YBSWJ, 5(13):67–89. For a description of Bluntschli's thought, see F. W. Coker, "Organismic Theories of the State: Nineteenth-Century Interpretations of the State as Organism or as Person," Ph.D. dissertation, Columbia University (New York: 1910), pp. 104–114.

6. See, for example, Edward Allen Kent, ed., *Law and Philosophy: Readings in Legal Philosophy* (Englewood Cliffs, N.J.: Prentice-Hall, 1970); Ronald Dworkin, *Taking Rights Seriously*, paperback ed. (Cambridge: Harvard University Press, 1978); J. Roland Pennock, "Rights, Natural Rights, and Human Rights—A General View," in Pennock and John W. Chapman, eds., *Human Rights*, Nomos XXIII, pp. 1–28 (New York: New York University Press, 1981); David Sidorsky, "Contemporary Reinterpretations of the Concept of Human Rights," in Sidorsky, ed., in collaboration with Sidney Liskofsky and Jerome J. Shestack, *Essays on Human Rights: Contemporary Issues and Jewish Perspectives*, pp. 88–109 (Philadelphia: Jewish Publication Society of America, 1979); *International Encyclopedia of the Social Sciences*, David L. Sills, ed. (New York: Macmillan and Free Press, 1968), 1:471–473.

7. Norbert Meienberger, *The Emergence of Constitutional Government in China (1905–1908)* (Bern: Peter Lang, 1980), pp. 26–38.

8. Cited in Meienberger, *ibid.*, pp. 84–85.

9. W. Y. Tsao, *The Constitutional Structure of Modern China* (Carlton, Victoria: Melbourne University Press, 1947), p. 57.

10. Zhang Foquan, *Ziyou yu renquan*, reprint ed. (Taibei: Quanguo chubanshe, 1979; first published 1954), passim, especially pp. 75–82, 252, 255.

11. Xiang Chunyi, Yang Jingyu, and Gu Angren, "Strive to Establish a Socialist Legal System with Chinese Characteristics," *Red Flag*, no. 3 (February 1, 1984), in Joint Publications Research Service (hereafter cited as JPRS), JPRS-CRF-84-006:11; quotation edited.

12. *Red Flag* quotation from Gu Chunde, "Lüe lun 'tianfu renquan' shuo," *Hongqi* (April 1, 1982), 7:35; "content of civil rights" quoted from Beijing Xinhua Domestic Service in Chinese, June 19, 1979, in FBIS, June 20, 1979, p. L8.

13. Zhu Jiamu, "Correctly Understand and Exercise the Right to Freedom of Speech," *Gongren ribao*, March 16, 1981, p. 3, in FBIS, March 30, 1981, p. L14; quotation corrected.

14. Wu Jingxiong, *Falü zhexue yanjiu*, second printing (Shanghai: Huiwentang xin shuju, 1937), p. 45.

15. Tao Xijin, "Some Questions Concerning the Drafting of Civil Law," excerpted from *Minzhu yu fazhi*, no. 9 (1981), in *Renmin ribao*, October 13, 1981, p. 5, in Foreign Broadcast Information Service (hereafter FBIS), October 21, 1981, quotation from p. K6.

16. See Andrew J. Nathan, *Chinese Democracy* (New York: Knopf, 1985), chapter 2.

17. Gerd Ruge, "An Interview with Chinese Legal Officials," *China Quarterly* (March 1975), 61:119.

18. Hungdah Chiu, "Socialist Legalism: Reform and Continuity in Post-Mao Communist China," *Issues and Studies* (November 1981), 17 (11):45–57.

19. *Renmin ribao*, April 8, 1984, p. 1.

20. For example, Zhang Jinqing and Xie Bangyu, "Independent Administering of Justice and the Leadership of the Communist Party," *Faxue yanjiu*, no. 2 (April 23, 1980), in JPRS, 76527:1–5; Lin Yicui, "Dang bixu zai xianfa he falü de fanwei nei huodong de jige wenti," *Renmin ribao*, March 28, 1983, p. 5.

21. Zhang Xin, "Enforcement of Policies and Enforcement of Laws," *Guangming ribao*, November 10, 1979, p. 3, in FBIS, November 14, 1979, pp. L1–L2.

22. Chen Shouyi and Zhang Hongsheng, chief eds., *Faxue jichu lilun* (Beijing: Beijing daxue chubanshe, 1981), p. 231.

23. Ming-min Peng, "Political Offenses in Taiwan: Laws and Problems," *China Quarterly* (July/September 1971), 47:471–480.

24. Chiu, "Socialist Legalism," pp. 69–72.

25. Cao Siyuan, "Ten Proposals for Revising the Constitution," *Minzhu yu fazhi*, no. 2 (February 20, 1981), in JPRS, 78412:7.

26. See, for example, Chen Yunsheng, "Lun xianfa baozhang," *Renmin ribao*, December 27, 1982, p. 5; Xiao Weiyun, "Lun xianfa shishi baozhang," *Faxue yanjiu* (June 23, 1982), 3:21–24.

27. "Criminal Law of the People's Republic of China," in FBIS, July 27, 1979, supplement 019, pp. 33–62; article 90, translation corrected.

28. Cf. Ouyang Tao and Yuan Zuoxi, "Tantan tong fan'geming xuanchuan fandong zui zuo douzheng de jige wenti," *Faxue yanjiu*, no. 2 (April 23, 1982), pp. 13–17; Li Wenyan, "How To Correctly Determine a Counterrevolutionary Purpose," *Guangming ribao*, August 20, 1983, p. 3, in FBIS, September 1, 1983, pp. K13–K15.

29. On the Wei case, see, e.g., "Unofficial Transcript of the Trial of Wei Jingsheng," Amnesty International Document ASA 17/01/80. On the problem of defining counterrevolution in general, see Ellen R. Eliasoph and Susan Gruneberg, "Law on Display in China," *China Quarterly* (December 1981), 88:677–680.

30. Ye Zi, "Is There Absolute Freedom of Speech?" *Hongqi*, no. 7 (April 1, 1981), in FBIS, April 27, 1981, p. K19.

31. Chen Weidian and Zhou Xinming, "Socialist Law Does Not Give Counterrevolutionaries Freedom of Speech," *Beijing ribao*, May 25, 1981, p. 3, in FBIS, June 12, 1981, pp. K10–K15.

32. On diaries, see Chen Xiulang, "Riji he zui!" *Renmin ribao*, August 4, 1979, p. 6. For an example of diary entries being used to prove counterrevolutionary intent, see Shanghai City Service in Mandarin, September 24, 1983, in FBIS, September 26, 1983, pp. 03–04. For other discussions concerning what should be the protected realm of free speech, see Sun Ruiyuan and Li Yanchi, "Socialist States Cannot Become Involved in 'Ideological Offenses,' " *Beijing ribao*, August 4, 1979, p. 3, in JPRS, 74286:1–3; He Lanjie, "Renzhen xuexi xingfa, yange zhixing xingfa," *Renmin ribao*, September 5, 1979, p. 3; Guo Luoji, "Political Questions Can Be Discussed," *Renmin ribao*, November 14, 1979, p. 3, in FBIS, November 19, 1979, pp. L7–L13; Shao Huaze, "Allow Full Play to Democracy in Theoretical Research," *Zhexue yanjiu* (March 25, 1979), 3:3–8, in JPRS, 73862: 62–70; Zhou Qiyu, "Another Talk on Freedom in Academic Studies," *Guangming ribao*, February 27, 1980, p. 3, in FBIS, March 7, 1980, pp. L4–L5; Cao, "Ten Proposals," pp. 5–6; Yeh Songting, "Dui 'yanzhe wu zui' de jidian kanfa," *Minzhu yu fazhi* (1980), 4:18–20; Li Buyun and Zhou Yuanqing, "Falü yu ziyou," *Hongqi* (November 16, 1981), 22:16–19.

33. Yang Xingfeng, "Yao buyao zhiding baozhang yanlun ziyou de falü?" *Minzhu yu fazhi* (1980), 9:6, replying to the article by Yeh Songting cited in note 32.

34. Among many examples, see Shanghai City Service in Mandarin, September 16, 1979, in FBIS, September 17, 1979, pp. 07–08; and Hefei Anhui Provincial Service, February 3, 1980, in FBIS, February 6, 1980, pp. 01–02.

35. Among many examples, see "Youli ye buyao qu'nao," *Renmin ribao*, November 22, 1979, p. 1; "Jie shangfang mingyi wuli qu'naozhe shoudao zhicai," *Renmin ribao*, December 11, 1979, p. 4; "Wuli qu'nao, faji burong," *Wenhui bao*, September 4, 1981, p. 4; "Shanxi kuangyuan ganbu Zhang Tao bei laojiao liangnian," *Renmin ribao*, September 23, 1981, p. 3.

36. Beijing Xinhua in English, May 23, 1984, in FBIS, May 24, 1984, p. K13.

37. Jerome Alan Cohen, *The Criminal Process in the People's Republic of China, 1949–1963: An Introduction* (Cambridge: Harvard University Press, 1968), p. 249.

38. Nathan, *Chinese Democracy*, chapters 2, 10.

39. Chiu, "Socialist Legalism," pp. 49–50.

40. Donald J. Munro, *The Concept of Man in Contemporary China* (Ann Arbor: University of Michigan Press, 1977), p. 162. Also see Thomas A. Metzger, *Escape from Predicament: Neo-Confucianism and China's Evolving Political Culture* (New York: Columbia University Press, 1977).

41. Hsieh Yu-Wei, "The Status of the Individual in Chinese Ethics," in Charles A. Moore, ed., with the assistance of Aldyth W. Morris, *The Status of the Individual in East and West*, p. 280 (Honolulu: University of Hawaii Press, 1968).

42. Derk Bodde, *China's Cultural Tradition: What and Whither?* reprint ed. (New York: Holt, Rinehart and Winston, 1966), p. 66.

43. Laurence A. Schneider, *A Madman of Ch'u: The Chinese Myth of Loyalty and Dissent* (Berkeley: University of California Press, 1980); Frederick W. Mote, "Confucian Eremitism in the Yüan Period," in Arthur F. Wright, ed., *The Confucian Persuasion*, pp. 202–240 (Stanford: Stanford University Press, 1960); Tu Wei-ming, *Neo-Confucian Thought in Action: Wang Yang-ming's Youth (1472–1509)* (Berkeley: University of California Press, 1976).

44. Wm. Theodore deBary, "A Plan for the Prince: The *Ming-i tai-fang lu* of Huang Tsung-hsi Translated and Explained," Ph.D. dissertation, Columbia University, 1953, especially pp. 208–211.

45. *YBSWJ*, 1(1):99.

46. *YBSWJ*, 2(5):49.

47. *YBSWJ*, 2(4):56–58.

48. Chang, *Liang Ch'i-ch'ao*, pp. 168–177 and elsewhere; Benjamin Schwartz, *In Search of Wealth and Power: Yen Fu and the West* (Cambridge: Harvard University Press, 1964), pp. 42–90. Also see James Reeve Pusey, *China and Charles Darwin* (Cambridge: Council on East Asian Studies, 1982).

49. Cited by Michael Gasster, *Chinese Intellectuals and the Revolution of 1911: The Birth of Modern Chinese Radicalism* (Seattle: University of Washington Press, 1969), p. 177.

50. Cited by Jerome B. Grieder, *Hu Shih and the Chinese Renaissance: Liberalism in the Chinese Revolution, 1917–1937* (Cambridge: Harvard University Press, 1970), p. 95.

51. Translated in Ssu-yü Teng and John K. Fairbank, *China's Response to the West: A Documentary Survey, 1839–1923* (Cambridge: Harvard University Press, 1961), pp. 241–242.

52. Guo Moruo, *Moruo wenji* (Beijing: Renmin wenxue chubanshe, 1959), vol. 10, "Wenyi lunji xu," p. 3.

53. *Miscellany of Mao Tse-tung Thought* (1949–1968), part 2, JPRS, 61269-2:250.

54. Li Qi, "Benefit and Morality," *Zhexue yanjiu* (May 25, 1979), 5:24–32, in JPRS, 74625:32.

55. Ma Junqi, "Views on Public and Private Interests That Radiate with the Glory of Materialist Dialectics," *Hongqi* (May 19, 1980), 10:10–13, in JPRS, 76076:20.

56. Commentator, "From Patriotism to Communism," *Red Flag*, no. 4 (February 16, 1983), in JPRS, 83314:2.

57. Zhang Liangjie, "Be Concerned for Personal Interests, Oppose Individualism," *Renmin ribao*, April 20, 1979, p. 4, in JPRS, 73881:30.

58. Li Chuanshi and Li Hejiu, "On the Marxist View of Public and Private Interests," *Changjiang ribao*, March 3, 1981, in JPRS, 78120:23–24.

59. *Ibid.*, p. 25.

60. Liang Feng and Wang Xing, "Realization of Individual Rights Also Requires Party Leadership—Once Again on Relationship Between People's Democracy and Party Leadership," *Beijing ribao*, December 28, 1981, in JPRS, 80211:3.

61. *Beijing Review* (1979), 22(30):19–21.

62. Chen Yingci and Liang Heng, "Strange Injustice of Taihang," *Guangming ribao*, September 20, 1980, p. 3, in FBIS, October 7, 1980, pp. L11–L15.

63. "Wei zhenli er douzheng de hao bangyang," *Guangming ribao*, November 4, 1980, p. 1.

64. Compare, for example, the case of Jiang Lihua: "Yang Shuqin Voluntarily Rectifies Her Wrong Judgment on a Case," *Renmin ribao*, March 1, 1979, in FBIS, March 9, 1979, pp. E6–E8.

65. Li Maoguan, "Gongmin de ziyou he falü," *Faxue yanjiu,* no. 2 (April 23, 1981), p. 7.

66. Chiang Kai-shek, *China's Destiny and Chinese Economic Theory* (New York: Roy Publishers, 1947), pp. 165–166.

67. Ma Boxuan, "Lun geren zhengdang liyi," *Guangming ribao,* November 15, 1980, p. 3.

68. See note 35.

69. Zhu Jiamu, "Correctly Understand and Exercise the Right of Freedom of Speech," *Gongren ribao,* March 16, 1981, p. 3, in JPRS, 78083:29.

70. E.g., "Who Is Fu Yuehua?" Beijing Xinhua Domestic Service, January 6, 1980, in FBIS, January 9, 1980, pp. L10–L14.

71. E.g., Beijing Xinhua Domestic Service in Chinese, October 18, 1979, in FBIS, October 19, 1979, p. L2.

72. *Jiefang ribao,* January 12, 1980, p. 1, in FBIS, January 25, 1980, p. L1.

73. Liang and Wang, "Realization of Individual Rights," p. 3 (see n. 60).

74. Zhang Huanguang, "On the Vital Significance of the Draft of the Revised Constitution to Perfecting the Government Administration Structure," *Guangming ribao,* May 19, 1982, p. 3, in FBIS, May 28, 1982, p. K10.

75. *Mao Zedong sixiang wansui* (1969), reprint ed. ([Taibei]: no publisher, no date), p. 667.

76. Wang Furu, "The Four Modernizations and Socialist Democracy," *Hongqi,* no. 4 (April 3, 1979), in JPRS, 73650:28.

77. Li and Zhou, "Falü yu ziyou," p. 19 (see n. 32).

78. The following discussion is based chiefly on Jin Yaoji, *Zhongguo minben sixiang zhi shi di fazhan* (Taibei: Jiaxin shuini gongsi wenhua jijinhui, 1964); Wang Erhmin, *Wan Qing zhengzhi sixiang shilun* (Taibei: Huashi chubanshe, 1969), ch. 9; Wei Zhengtong, *Chuantong yu xiandaihua* (Taibei: Shuiniu chubanshe, 1968), pp. 111–142; Zhou Daoqi, "Woguo minben sixiang de fenxi yu jiantao," *Guoji Hanxue huiyi lunwen ji, Sixiang yu zhexue zu* (Taibei: Zhongyang yanjiu yuan, 1981), 2:951–994.

79. The quotations are, in order, from the following books, parts, and chapters of *Mencius*: 1:1:6, 1:1:3, 1:2:10, 1:2:7, 1:2:8, and 7:2:14. The translations are adapted from Arthur Waley, *Three Ways of Thought in Ancient China* (Garden City, N.Y.: Doubleday Anchor, no date), and James Legge, *The Chinese Classics,* 5 vols. (Hong Kong: Hong Kong University Press, 1960), vol. 2.

80. Examples taken from Wang, *Wan Qing,* pp. 234–235 (see n. 78).

81. *Ibid.,* pp. 240–241.

82. Philip A. Kuhn, "Local Self-Government Under the Republic: Problems of Control, Autonomy, and Mobilization," in Frederick Wakeman, Jr., and Carolyn Grant, eds., *Conflict and Control in Late Imperial China,* pp. 261–275 (Berkeley: University of California Press, 1975); Judith Anne Whitbeck, "Averting Dynastic Decline: Political Ethics in Kung Tzu-chen's Reform Thought," paper presented to the Modern China Seminar, Columbia University, October 9, 1980.

83. Examples taken from Wang, *Wan Qing,* pp. 236–238.

84. Kang Youwei, "Qing ding lixian kai guohui zhe," in Jian Bozan et al., comps., *Wuxu bianfa* (Shanghai: Renmin chubanshe, 1961), 2:236.

85. Chang, *Liang Ch'i-ch'ao,* p. 201 (see n. 4); order of sentences altered.

86. *Ibid.,* p. 100.

87. Sun Yat-sen, *San Min Chu I, The Three Principles of the People,* Frank W. Price, trans., L. T. Chen, ed., reprint ed. (New York: Da Capo Press, 1975), pp. 342–343.

88. Mao Zedong, "Speeches at the Supreme State Conference," *Chinese Law and Government* (Fall 1976), 9(3):84.

89. Hua Guofeng, "Report on the Work of the Government," June 18, 1979, in *Beijing Review* (1979), 22(27):22.

90. There has been some debate in recent years over whether democracy is among the ends of socialism, but the official view remains that it is only a means. See, for example, Lu Zhichao, "Democracy is Both a Means and an End," *Zhexue yanjiu*, no. 12 (December 25, 1980), in JPRS, 77613:19–31.

91. Interview with Peng Zhen by *Liaowang*, no. 5 (May 20, 1982), reprinted in *Renmin ribao*, May 21, 1982, p. 3.

92. *The Works of Jeremy Bentham*, John Bowring, ed. (New York: Russell and Russell, 1962), 2:501.

93. *YBSWJ*, 5(13):30–47. The first quotation below from this essay is slightly reordered; the second follows Chang, *Liang Ch'i-ch'ao*, p. 207 (see n. 4).

94. Schwartz, *In Search of Wealth*, pp. 136, 141.

95. Luo Longji, "Lun renquan," in Liang Shiqiu, Hu Shi, and Luo Longji, *Renquan lunji* (Shanghai: Xinyue shudian, 1930), pp. 33–73.

96. *YBSWJ*, 6(17):21.

97. Sun, *San Min*, p. 210 (see n. 87).

98. Cited in Lloyd E. Eastman, *The Abortive Revolution: China Under Nationalist Rule, 1927–1937* (Cambridge: Harvard University Press, 1974), p. 149.

99. Grieder, *Hu Shih and the Chinese Renaissance*, pp. 266–268.

100. Zhu, "Correctly Understand," p. L13 (see n. 69).

101. Shang Zhe, "Persistently Carry Forward Socialist Democracy," *Hongqi*, no. 6 (June 1, 1979), pp. 44–50, in JPRS 73956: 83–84, quotation slightly edited.

102. Xinhua contributing commentator, "Keep to the Correct Orientation of Socialist Democracy," Beijing Xinhua Domestic Service in Chinese, January 20, 1980, in FBIS, January 22, 1980, p. L7.

103. Xiao Wang and Lao Zhou, "The Allegory of Playing Basketball," Shanghai City Service in Mandarin, April 9, 1979, in FBIS, April 11, 1979, p. O8.

104. "Hu Qiaomu tongzhi zai Beijing xinwenxuehui chengli dahuishang de jianghua," *Xinwen zhanxian*, no. 4 (April 1980), p. 8.

105. Bentham, *Works*, 1:29–30; John Stuart Mill, "On Liberty," in *The Utilitarians*, paperback ed. (Garden City, N.Y.: Dolphin Books, 1961), p. 485.

106. Liang Qichao, *Xin dalu youji jielu*, reprint ed. (Taibei: Zhonghua shuju, 1957), especially pp. 122–123.

107. Guy S. Alitto, *The Last Confucian: Liang Shu-ming and the Chinese Dilemma of Modernity* (Berkeley: University of California Press, 1979), pp. 192–225.

108. See, for example, Chiang, *China's Destiny*, pp. 183–213.

109. "Text of Deng's Report on Current Situation, Tasks," *Zhengming*, no. 29 (March 1, 1980), in FBIS, March 11, 1980, supplement, p. 23.

110. Jia Chunfeng and Teng Wensheng, "Strive to Overcome the 'Traces That Have Yet to be Overcome'—On Eliminating the Remnant Influence of Feudalism," *Renmin ribao*, October 9, 1980, p. 5, in FBIS, October 22, 1980, quotation from p. L12.

111. Zhang Xianyang and Wang Guixin, "Wuchan jieji minzhu he zichan jieji minzhu," *Renmin ribao*, June 9, 1979, p. 2.

112. The most recent of the many works by Wm. Theodore deBary addressing these questions is *The Liberal Tradition in China* (Hong Kong: Chinese University Press, 1983).

113. Translation from Hualing Nieh, ed., *Literature of the Hundred Flowers*, vol. 2, *Poetry and Fiction* (New York: Columbia University Press, 1981), pp. 308–309. For publication date and Chinese text see Feng Xuefeng, *Xuefeng wenji* (Beijing: Renmin wenxue chubanshe, 1981), vol. 1, "Diyijuan shuoming" and p. 470. On Feng's fate, see *Chinese Literature* (March 1980), pp. 12–13.

114. See Nathan, *Chinese Democracy*, especially ch. 5.

115. For example, Xu Chongde, "Bourgeois Universal Suffrage Is a Fraud," *Beijing ribao*, June 1, 1979, p. 3, in FBIS, June 13, 1979, pp. L2–L3; Chen Jun, "American Elections," *Beijing ribao*, January 23, 1981, p. 3, in JPRS, 77590:1–4; Tan Guochen, "Is There Press Freedom in the United States?" *Guangming ribao*, April 17, 1981, p. 3, in FBIS, May 4, 1981, pp. B3–B6.

116. See, *inter alia*, Shen Baoxiang, Wang Chengquan, and Li Zerui, "Guanyu guoji lingyu de renquan wenti," *Hongqi* (April 16, 1982), 8:44–48; Hao Ru, "Renquan de lishi he xianzhuang," *Renmin Ribao*, April 13, 1982, p. 5; *Beijing Review* (1982), 25(30):13–17, 22.

For Further Reading

This is a selective list of materials available in English for those who wish more information about the current state and historical background of rights in China.

Bao Ruo-wang (Jean Pasqualini) and Rudolph Chelminski. *Prisoner of Mao.* Harmondsworth, Middlesex: Penguin, 1976. An autobiographical account of seven years in Chinese labor camps.

Beijing Review. A weekly Chinese government magazine for foreign readers that carries occasional articles on Chinese law and Chinese views on international and domestic rights issues. The text of the current constitution may be found in no. 52, 1982.

Derk Bodde and Clarence Morris. *Law in Imperial China: Exemplified by 190 Ch'ing Dynasty Cases (Translated from the Hsing-an hui-lan) with Historical, Social, and Juridical Commentaries.* Cambridge: Harvard University Press, 1967. The most complete and detailed account in English of the theory and practice of criminal law in late imperial times.

China: Violations of Human Rights, Prisoners of Conscience, and the Death Penalty in the People's Republic of China. London: Amnesty International, 1984. Details Amnesty's charges that as of the mid-1980s the PRC continues to imprison political and religious dissidents, and presents Amnesty's case against the use of the death penalty in China.

"China's Legal Development." Special issue of *Columbia Journal of Transnational Law* (1983), vol. 22, no. 1. Articles on such topics as the growth of China's legal system, legal aspects of foreign economic relations, and legal education, mostly by leading Chinese legal scholars; includes an annotated bibliography of source and secondary materials, chiefly in English, emphasizing materials relevant to China's foreign trade.

"Chinese Criminal Law Symposium." *Journal of Criminal Law and Criminology* (Spring 1982), 73(1):135–316. Includes the texts of the 1979 criminal law and criminal procedure law and three scholarly commentaries on aspects of the codes.

Jerome Alan Cohen. *The Criminal Process in the People's Republic of China, 1949–1963: An Introduction.* Cambridge: Harvard University Press, 1968. Although this book predates the 1979 criminal and criminal procedure laws, the sanctioning procedures it describes are still in use, as are most of the laws and regulations it analyzes.

R. Randle Edwards. "Reflections on Crime and Punishment in China, with Appended Sentencing Documents." *Columbia Journal of Transnational Law* (1977), 16(1):45–103. An analysis of the principles involved in deciding criminal sentences in the early 1970s.

——comp. "Law in People's China." 7 vols., photocopied. New York: Columbia Law School, 1984. Selections from the Chinese press and from scholarly works covering all aspects of Chinese law, compiled for use in courses at Columbia Law School. Available from the Center for Chinese Legal Studies, Columbia Law School.

Raymond D. Gastil, ed. *Freedom in the World: Political Rights and Civil Liberties, 1983–1984.* Westport: Greenwood Press, 1984. This issue of Freedom House's yearbook contains a section entitled "Supporting the Development of Democracy in China," with eight papers and the transcript of a conference on the subject.

Merle Goldman. "Human Rights in the People's Republic of China." *Daedalus* (Fall 1983), 112(4):111–138. The form human rights issues have taken in various movements of dissent in Communist China.

Shao-chuan Leng and Hungdah Chiu. *Criminal Justice in Post-Mao China* (Albany: State University of New York Press, 1985). A fact-filled survey of the Chinese legal system with special reference to criminal justice, including court structure and procedure, the role of lawyers and the police, the legal definitions of various crimes, and sanctioning policy.

Liang Heng and Judith Shapiro. *Intellectual Freedom in China After Mao, with a Focus on 1983.* New York: Fund for Free Expression, 1984. The limits of artistic freedom and the mechanisms of control since Mao's death.

Fu-shun Lin, comp. and ed. *Chinese Law Past and Present: A Bibliography of Enactments and Commentaries in English Text.* New York: East Asian Institute, Columbia University, 1966. Provides control of the English-language literature on Chinese Communist law up to the eve of the Cultural Revolution; as yet, no similar research guide exists for the post-Mao flowering of Chinese law, but see the entry under Jeanette L. Pinard.

Andrew J. Nathan. *Chinese Democracy.* New York: Knopf, 1985. A history of Chinese ideas about the relationship between citizen and state since late imperial times and an analysis of the impact of the political reforms of the early 1980s.

Jeanette L. Pinard. *The People's Republic of China: A Bibliography of Selected*

English-Language Legal Materials. Washington, D.C.: Library of Congress Law Library, 1983. 72 pp. Provides guidance to secondary and English-language primary sources on all fields of Chinese law in the late 1970s and early 1980s.

Political Imprisonment in the People's Republic of China. London: Amnesty International, 1978. Published before the legal reforms of recent years, the book describes the laws, judicial process, and prison system used against political (and other) crimes in the later part of Mao's life. See *China: Violations of Human Rights* for a more recent Amnesty report.

Allyn and Adele Rickett. *Prisoners of Liberation.* New York: Cameron Associates, 1957. Insight into Chinese ways of thinking about law and penology from two American China scholars who were imprisoned in China for several years in the early 1950s.

James D. Seymour, ed. *The Fifth Modernization: China's Human Rights Movement, 1978–1979.* Stanfordville, N.Y.: Coleman, 1980. Texts of posters and publications emanating from the short-lived but revealing Democracy Wall movement.

——*China Rights Annals, 1: Human Rights Developments in the People's Republic of China from October 1983 Through September 1984.* Armonk, N.Y.: Sharpe, 1985. Detailed account of recent developments in political, social, and economic rights, organized according to the categories of the Universal Declaration of Human Rights.

Susan L. Shirk. "Human Rights—What About China?" *Foreign Policy* (Winter 1977–1978), 29:109–127. Analyzes potential sources of dissent in China and advocates including the PRC within the ambit of U.S. human rights policy.

SPEAHRhead: Bulletin of the Society for the Protection of East Asians' Human Rights. (1979–1984), nos. 1–20. This journal carried articles, detailed information, and documentary excerpts on human rights developments in China and other Asian countries.

Robert G. Sutter. "Human Rights in China." Congressional Research Service, Library of Congress. (February 8, 1978), 78–50F. 55 pp. A survey of human rights in China and discussion of different views on how human rights should figure in American China policy.

Ross Terrill, ed. *The China Difference.* New York: Harper and Row, 1970. Interpretive essays on Chinese values, seen in contrast to American values; includes chapters on Chinese human rights values, on due process in Chinese law, and on ideas of privacy, self-expression, and other rights-related issues.

For materials on human rights generally, including studies of human rights in selected countries and regions, see *Human Rights: A Topical Bibliography*, comp. by the Center for the Study of Human Rights, Columbia University (Boulder, Colo.: Westview Press, 1983); Louis Henkin, *The Rights of Man Today* (Boulder, Colo.: Westview Press, 1978); and A. H. Robertson, *Human Rights in the World*, 2d ed. (Manchester: Manchester University Press, 1982).

Index

188 **Index**

Compensation, right to, 94, 103, 111, 117, 121, 144, 145

Confucianism, 2, 79, 111, 127, 140, 148–49, 155; and the individual, 21, 44, 138–39, 142, 143; *see also* Neo-Confucianism

Constitution, U.S., 13, 15, 16, 17, 18, 19; and Chinese constitutions, 26, 27, 122–24

Constitutionalism, 7, 13, 23, 46, 47, 78–79, 125, 151–52; *see also particular constitutions*

Constitutional Principles of the Shaan-Gan-Ning Border Region (1946), 57, 71–72, 100, 101, 173n40

Constitution of 1923 (republic), 80–81, 86–89, 93

Constitution of 1946 (GMD), 80–81, 93–96, 99, 130, 131, 133, 146

Constitution of 1954 (PRC), 24, 102–9, 134; civil rights in, 55, 57, 80–81; economic rights in, 68, 70, 72, 73; and other constitutions, 110, 119

Constitution of 1975 (PRC), 24, 109–12, 132; civil rights in, 57, 59, 80–81, 100; economic rights in, 68, 69, 70, 72; and other constitutions, 102, 105, 113, 114, 115, 116, 119

Constitution of 1978 (PRC), 48, 99, 109, 112–15; civil rights in, 57, 59, 66, 80–81, 117, 166n17, 167n8; economic rights in, 68, 69, 70, 72; and other constitutions, 102, 105, 116, 117, 118, 119, 120

Constitution of 1982 (PRC), 24–26, 30–33, 48–52, 59, 102, 109, 115–120, 146, 154; civil rights in, 55, 56, 57, 58–59, 60–61, 167n17; and law, 63, 66, 134, 166n9; economic rights in, 68, 69, 70–71, 72, 73

Constitutions, Chinese: rights in, 3, 5, 35, 57, 58, 60–61, 80–81, 82, 164; Western influence on, 23, 48, 122, 124, 126, 129; nature of, 24, 27, 120–24, 130–31, 143, 164; and law, 47–52, 60, 63, 126, 131–37, 153, 166nn9,10, 168n12, 175n75; and the individual, 55, 144, 145, 148, 160, 161; and economic rights, 67, 70, 153; of CCP, 101, 108; evolution of, 120, 125, 146; *see also* Common Program of

1949; Draft Outline Fundamental Law of the Chinese Soviet Government; Jiangxi Program; Principles of the Constitution; Provisional Constitution; Provisional Constitution for the Tutelage Period; Temple of Heaven Draft of 1913

Correspondence, freedom of, 80, 87, 90, 93; under CCP, 59–60, 100, 103, 107, 111, 117, 135

Criminal process: and international standards, 9, 63; Chinese view of, 47, 62, 74; and rights, 44, 58, 63–66, 106, 116, 134–36, 166n15; under GMD, 91, 94; *see also* Equality before the law; Legal system

Culture, freedom of, 81, 121, 136, 168n26; in GMD constitution, 92, 93; in PRC constitutions, 103, 110, 113, 117–18

Cultural Revolution, 2, 72; and Chinese constitution, 24, 51, 109; rights in, 35, 38, 73, 110, 167n8; abuses in, 56, 61, 145, 160, 164, 169n36; deprivation of rights in, 74, 106, 133–34

Darwinism, Social, 140, 141, 150

Death penalty, 44, 64

de Bary, Wm. Theodore, 127

Declaration of Independence (U.S.), 10, 126

Declaration of the Rights of Man and of the Citizen (France), 10

Democracy, 12, 77; and Chinese tradition, 20, 150, 151, 153; in PRC, 24, 106, 113; purpose of, 33, 152, 158–59, 181n90; socialist, 49, 51, 78, 101, 102, 146, 147, 159–60; Chinese desire for, 61, 160; and GMD, 89–90; bourgeois, 145, 147, 159, 163; in U.S., 161, 162; *see also* Democracy Movement

Democracy and the Legal System, 51, 131

Democracy Movement, 51, 102, 113, 131, 160; activists in, 135, 136, 144–45, 169n33; *see also* Peking Spring Movement

Democracy Wall, 3, 49, 160

Democratic centralism, 25, 29, 32

Demonstration, freedom of, 81, 103, 107, 110, 121, 123, 136

Deng Xiaoping, 49, 112, 115, 159, 166n11, 169n32

Studies of the East Asian Institute

THE LADDER OF SUCCESS IN IMPERIAL CHINA, by Ping-ti Ho. New York: Columbia University Press, 1962.

THE CHINESE INFLATION, 1937–1949, by Shun-hsin Chou. New York: Columbia University Press, 1963.

REFORMER IN MODERN CHINA: CHANG CHIEN, 1853–1926, by Samuel Chu. New York: Columbia University Press, 1965.

RESEARCH IN JAPANESE SOURCES: A GUIDE, by Herschel Webb with the assistance of Marleigh Ryan. New York: Columbia University Press, 1965.

SOCIETY AND EDUCATION IN JAPAN, by Herbert Passin. New York: Teachers College Press, 1965.

AGRICULTURAL PRODUCTION AND ECONOMIC DEVELOPMENT IN JAPAN, 1873–1922, by James I. Nakamura. Princeton: Princeton University Press, 1966.

JAPAN'S FIRST MODERN NOVEL: UKIGUMO OF FUTABATEI SHIMEI, by Marleigh Ryan. New York: Columbia University Press, 1967.

THE KOREAN COMMUNIST MOVEMENT, 1918–1948, by Dae-Sook Suh. Princeton: Princeton University Press, 1967.

THE FIRST VIETNAM CRISIS, by Melvin Gurtov. New York: Columbia University Press, 1967.

CADRES, BUREAUCRACY, AND POLITICAL POWER IN COMMUNIST CHINA, by A. Doak Barnett. New York: Columbia University Press, 1968.

THE JAPANESE IMPERIAL INSTITUTION IN THE TOKUGAWA PERIOD, by Herschel Webb. New York: Columbia University Press, 1968.

HIGHER EDUCATION AND BUSINESS RECRUITMENT IN JAPAN, by Koya Azumi. New York: Teachers College Press, 1969.

THE COMMUNISTS AND PEASANT REBELLIONS: A STUDY IN THE REWRIT-
ING OF CHINESE HISTORY, by James P. Harrison, Jr. New York: Atheneum,
1969.
HOW THE CONSERVATIVES RULE JAPAN, by Nathaniel B. Thayer. Princeton:
Princeton University Press, 1969.
ASPECTS OF CHINESE EDUCATION, edited by C. T. Hu. New York: Teachers
College Press, 1970.
DOCUMENTS OF KOREAN COMMUNISM, 1918–1948, by Dae-Sook Suh.
Princeton: Princeton University Press, 1970.
JAPANESE EDUCATION: A BIBLIOGRAPHY OF MATERIALS IN THE ENGLISH
LANGUAGE, by Herbert Passin. New York: Teachers College Press, 1970.
ECONOMIC DEVELOPMENT AND THE LABOR MARKET IN JAPAN, by Koji
Taira. New York: Columbia University Press, 1970.
THE JAPANESE OLIGARCHY AND THE RUSSO-JAPANESE WAR, by Shumpei
Okamoto. New York: Columbia University Press, 1970.
IMPERIAL RESTORATION IN MEDIEVAL JAPAN, by H. Paul Varley. New York:
Columbia University Press, 1971.
JAPAN'S POSTWAR DEFENSE POLICY, 1947–1968, by Martin E. Weinstein.
New York: Columbia University Press, 1971.
ELECTION CAMPAIGNING JAPANESE STYLE, by Gerald L. Curtis. New York:
Columbia University Press, 1971.
CHINA AND RUSSIA: THE "GREAT GAME," by O. Edmund Clubb. New York:
Columbia University Press, 1971.
MONEY AND MONETARY POLICY IN COMMUNIST CHINA, by Katharine Huang
Hsiao. New York: Columbia University Press, 1971.
THE DISTRICT MAGISTRATE IN LATE IMPERIAL CHINA, by John R. Watt. New
York: Columbia University Press, 1972.
LAW AND POLICY IN CHINA'S FOREIGN RELATIONS: A STUDY OF ATTITUDE
AND PRACTICE, by James C. Hsiung. New York: Columbia University Press,
1972.
PEARL HARBOR AS HISTORY: JAPANESE-AMERICAN RELATIONS, 1931–1941,
edited by Dorothy Borg and Shumpei Okamoto, with the assistance of Dale
K. A. Finlayson. New York: Columbia University Press, 1973.
JAPANESE CULTURE: A SHORT HISTORY, by H. Paul Varley. New York: Prae-
ger, 1973.
DOCTORS IN POLITICS: THE POLITICAL LIFE OF THE JAPAN MEDICAL AS-
SOCIATION, by William E. Steslicke. New York: Praeger, 1973.
THE JAPAN TEACHERS UNION: A RADICAL INTEREST GROUP IN JAPANESE
POLITICS, by Donald Ray Thurston. Princeton: Princeton University Press,
1973.
JAPAN'S FOREIGN POLICY, 1868–1941: A RESEARCH GUIDE, edited by James
William Morley. New York: Columbia University Press, 1974.
PALACE AND POLITICS IN PREWAR JAPAN, by David Anson Titus. New York:
Columbia University Press, 1974.

THE IDEA OF CHINA: ESSAYS IN GEOGRAPHIC MYTH AND THEORY, by Andrew March. Devon, England: David and Charles, 1974.

ORIGINS OF THE CULTURAL REVOLUTION, by Roderick MacFarquhar. New York: Columbia University Press, 1974.

SHIBA KŌKAN: ARTIST, INNOVATOR, AND PIONEER IN THE WESTERNIZATION OF JAPAN, by Calvin L. French. Tokyo: Weatherhill, 1974.

INSEI: ABDICATED SOVEREIGNS IN THE POLITICS OF LATE HEIAN JAPAN, by G. Cameron Hurst. New York: Columbia University Press, 1975.

EMBASSY AT WAR, by Harold Joyce Noble. Edited with an introduction by Frank Baldwin, Jr. Seattle: University of Washington Press, 1975.

REBELS AND BUREAUCRATS; CHINA'S DECEMBER 9ERS, by John Israel and Donald W. Klein. Berkeley: University of California Press, 1975.

DETERRENT DIPLOMACY, edited by James William Morley. New York: Columbia University Press, 1976.

HOUSE UNITED, HOUSE DIVIDED: THE CHINESE FAMILY IN TAIWAN, by Myron L. Cohen. New York: Columbia University Press, 1976.

ESCAPE FROM PREDICAMENT: NEO-CONFUCIANISM AND CHINA'S EVOLVING POLITICAL CULTURE, by Thomas A. Metzger. New York: Columbia University Press, 1976.

CADRES, COMMANDERS, AND COMMISSARS: THE TRAINING OF THE CHINESE COMMUNIST LEADERSHIP, 1920–45, by Jane L. Price. Boulder, Colo.: Westview Press, 1976.

SUN YAT-SEN: FRUSTRATED PATRIOT, by C. Martin Wilbur. New York: Columbia University Press, 1977.

JAPANESE INTERNATIONAL NEGOTIATING STYLE, by Michael Blaker. New York: Columbia University Press, 1977.

CONTEMPORARY JAPANESE BUDGET POLITICS, by John Creighton Campbell. Berkeley: University of California Press, 1977.

THE MEDIEVAL CHINESE OLIGARCHY, by David Johnson. Boulder, Colo.: Westview Press, 1977.

THE ARMS OF KIANGNAN: MODERNIZATION IN THE CHINESE ORDNANCE INDUSTRY, 1860–1895, by Thomas L. Kennedy. Boulder, Colo.: Westview Press, 1978.

PATTERNS OF JAPANESE POLICYMAKING: EXPERIENCES FROM HIGHER EDUCATION, by T. J. Pempel. Boulder, Colo.: Westview Press, 1978.

THE CHINESE CONNECTION: ROGER S. GREENE, THOMAS W. LAMONT, GEORGE E. SOKOLSKY, AND AMERICAN-EAST ASIAN RELATIONS, by Warren I. Cohen. New York: Columbia University Press, 1978.

MILITARISM IN MODERN CHINA: THE CAREER OF WU P'EI-FU, 1916–1939, by Odoric Y. K. Wou. Folkestone, England: Dawson, 1978.

A CHINESE PIONEER FAMILY: THE LINS OF WU-FENG, by Johanna Meskill. Princeton University Press, 1979.

PERSPECTIVES ON A CHANGING CHINA, edited by Joshua A. Fogel and William T. Rowe. Boulder, Colo.: Westview Press, 1979.

THE MEMOIRS OF LI TSUNG-JEN, by T. K. Tong and Li Tsung-jen. Boulder, Colo.: Westview Press, 1979.

UNWELCOME MUSE: CHINESE LITERATURE IN SHANGHAI AND PEKING, 1937–1945, by Edward Gunn. New York: Columbia University Press, 1979.

YENAN AND THE GREAT POWERS: THE ORIGINS OF CHINESE COMMUNIST FOREIGN POLICY, by James Reardon-Anderson. New York: Columbia University Press, 1980.

UNCERTAIN YEARS: CHINESE-AMERICAN RELATIONS, 1947–1950, edited by Dorothy Borg and Waldo Heinrichs. New York: Columbia University Press, 1980.

THE FATEFUL CHOICE: JAPAN'S ADVANCE INTO SOUTHEAST ASIA, edited by James William Morley. New York: Columbia University Press, 1980.

TANAKA GIICHI AND JAPAN'S CHINA POLICY, by William F. Morton. Folkestone, England: Dawson, 1980; New York: St. Martin's Press, 1980.

THE ORIGINS OF THE KOREAN WAR: LIBERATION AND THE EMERGENCE OF SEPARATE REGIMES, 1945–1947, by Bruce Cumings. Princeton University Press, 1981.

CLASS CONFLICT IN CHINESE SOCIALISM, by Richard Curt Kraus. New York: Columbia University Press, 1981.

EDUCATION UNDER MAO: CLASS AND COMPETITION IN CANTON SCHOOLS, by Jonathan Unger. New York: Columbia University Press, 1982.

PRIVATE ACADEMIES OF TOKUGAWA JAPAN, by Richard Rubinger. Princeton: Princeton University Press, 1982.

JAPAN AND THE SAN FRANCISCO PEACE SETTLEMENT, by Michael M. Yoshitsu. New York: Columbia University Press, 1982.

NEW FRONTIERS IN AMERICAN-EAST ASIAN RELATIONS: ESSAYS PRESENTED TO DOROTHY BORG, edited by Warren I. Cohen. New York: Columbia University Press, 1983.

THE ORIGINS OF THE CULTURAL REVOLUTION: II, THE GREAT LEAP FORWARD, 1958–1960, by Roderick MacFarquhar. New York: Columbia University Press, 1983.

THE CHINA QUAGMIRE: JAPAN'S EXPANSION ON THE ASIAN CONTINENT, 1933–1941, edited by James William Morley. New York: Columbia University Press, 1983.

FRAGMENTS OF RAINBOWS: THE LIFE AND POETRY OF SAITO MOKICHI, 1882–1953, by Amy Vladeck Heinrich. New York: Columbia University Press, 1983.

THE U.S.-SOUTH KOREAN ALLIANCE: EVOLVING PATTERNS OF SECURITY RELATIONS, edited by Gerald L. Curtis and Sung-joo Han. Lexington, Mass.: Lexington Books, 1983.

THE FOREIGN POLICY OF THE REPUBLIC OF KOREA, edited by Youngnok Koo and Sung-joo Han. New York: Columbia University Press, 1984.

JAPANESE CULTURE, third edition, revised, by Paul Varley. University of Hawaii Press, 1984.

JAPAN'S MODERN MYTHS: IDEOLOGY IN THE LATE MEIJI PERIOD, by Carol Gluck. Princeton: Princeton University Press, 1985.

SHAMANS, HOUSEWIVES, AND OTHER RESTLESS SPIRITS: WOMEN IN KO- REAN RITUAL LIFE, by Laurel Kendall. Honolulu: University of Hawaii Press, 1985.

HUMAN RIGHTS IN CONTEMPORARY CHINA, by R. Randle Edwards, Louis Henkin, and Andrew J. Nathan. New York: Columbia University Press, 1986.